CONCILIUM

concilium 1990/2

THE ETHICS OF WORLD RELIGIONS AND HUMAN RIGHTS

Edited by

Hans Küng and
Jürgen Moltmann

SCM Press · London
Trinity Press International · Philadelphia

April 1990

ISBN: 0 334 03001 3

Typeset at The Spartan Press Ltd, Lymington, Hants
Printed by Dotesios Printers Ltd, Trowbridge, Wilts

Concilium: Published February, April, June, August, October, December.

Contents

Editorial

Curiously enough, many of the great world religions have their problems with the affirmation and realization of human rights which were first proclaimed by the American and French Revolutions and finally grounded in the Declaration of Human Rights of the United Nations in 1948. The Popes of the nineteenth century condemned human rights as an expression of secularism, naturalism, indifferentism and laicism. Only the greatest ecumenical pope of our century, John XXIII, spoke in his encyclical *Pacem in Terris* (1963) unambiguously in favour of human rights and praised their proclamation by the United Nations as an 'act of the highest importance'.

The other world religions also have their own problems with human rights, especially with the rights of women and with the rights of other believers. But can one overlook the fact that, at the present time, all world religions are going through a process of affirming the complete range of human rights? Is it conceivable that in the future, world religions, in particular, will be the great supporters of human rights?

It would be of the utmost importance for humanity if the great world religions could agree upon a basic ethic and – following on from this ethic – upon basic rights of human beings. The declaration of the 'World Conference of Religions for Peace', held in Kyoto, Japan, in 1970 was only a beginning:

Meeting together to deal with the paramount theme of peace, we discovered that the things that unite us are more important than the things that divide us. We found that we have in common:
a conviction of the fundamental unity of the human family, of the equality and dignity of all men and women;
a sense of the sacrosanctness of the individual and his conscience;
a sense of the value of the human community;
a recognition that might is not the same as right, that human might cannot be self-sufficient and is not absolute;
the belief that love, compassion, selflessness and the power of mind and

inner truthfulness have, in the end, more power than hatred, enmity and self-interest;

a sense of obligation to stand on the side of the poor and oppressed against the rich and the oppressors;

deep hope that good will, in the end, will triumph.

The aim of this issue is that, from the perspective of each religion represented, two sets of questions should be considered:

1. How are human rights grounded in the tradition of each religion? What are the strong points in each tradition for the grounding and realization of human rights?

2. Where are the deficiencies in theory and practice in each religion? What are the weak points in the basis for and realization of human rights?

Unfortunately the promised contribution giving the Chinese position did not arrive in time. So as the question of human rights is a matter of particular dispute in Islam at the moment, we have included a second contribution on this religion. As both contributions shed light on different perspectives, they are able to complement each other well.

This issue demonstrates, on the whole, that awareness of the problem of human rights has increased in the different religions. With regard to a general basic ethos of world religions, on the other hand, our task is only beginning. This issue does, however, try to create awareness of the problem in just that respect.

Hans Küng
Jürgen Moltmann

Translated by Gordon Wood

Europe and the Gospel

Europe is in the making. Suddenly, faster than people expected. What Europe? Certainly a continent the riches of whose spiritual life are not at the level of its technological inventiveness and its prosperity. Europe is also the object of the churches' concern and even of a church strategy based on its Christian roots or its renewed openness to a proclamation of the gospel. Given such presuppositions, we may well feel some unease, since for the last fifty years only the most reactionary causes have made the claim that Europe is fundamentally Christian and that this Christian character must be defended as such. When it comes to the substance of Christianity, these crusades are content with very little. But such an analysis would need to be developed further elsewhere.

As for the gospel, we may indeed suppose that the 'Christianity' of former times is a myth. But sociologically it is true that it has represented a symbiosis between the church and civil society and that it has been characterized by institutions which have been mixtures of power and service, accompanied by multiple cultural exchanges in one direction or the other. Now that these institutions have managed to die, or almost die, it should be impossible to go on cherishing any illusion that our culture is impregnated with Christianity, except in the sense that there can be affinities between what Christians experience through the gospel and what others experience for different reasons. However, that is quite a different perspective.

If we want to use the criteria applied to representations current in official circles of the Catholic church in measuring this divorce, it has to be said that any idea that ethical or social teaching in conformity to doctrines received in this church carries the least credibility is sheer wishful thinking, however prestigious or even beloved the authorities may be who propose it. If there seems to be an agreement on 'human rights', it arises out of a permanent confusion between two very different conceptions, one relating to the political and social rights of the individual over against the state and the other relating to the religious rights of the individual. Finally, the conviction that elements of Christian culture in the narrowest sense of the term still persist clashes with the results of surveys which show a growing and absolutely staggering ignorance of the most basic religious knowledge.

If Europe tends to be a cultural *tabula rasa* as far as Christianity is concerned, can one at least count on its religious aspirations? On the one hand, the statistics speak volumes. In France, for example, while 25% of the population are Christians who practise regularly or occasionally, 50% of non-Christians or nominal Catholics are totally indifferent; the remaining 25% have a certain interest in Christianity, a certain sense of belonging to the church, but they do not accept either obligations or sanctions, nor do they have any allegiance to the commands or propositions pronounced with authority. On the other hand, concepts like a 'religious revival' or the existence of a 'post-modernity' more favourable to Christianity, which are drummed into our ears, are apologetic concepts forged for the needs of the cause. Those who talk of a 'religious revival' are lumping together pietistic movements within confessing or practising groups and a degree of renewed interest in religious questions in other circles from which it is impossible to tell whether Christian claims benefit. As for 'post-modernity', it is a delusion to believe that weariness or disillusionment at the ideals of progress and victorious rationality amount to a questioning of reason itself and its autonomy, which is generally called 'secularization'.

I know that it is the done thing in certain circles to think of Western Europe as having been debased by the heritage of the Enlightenment and its material prosperity, and to look for a decisive impetus from the arrival on the scene of Eastern Europe as it finds its religious freedom. We can only welcome and rejoice at the fact that in the East there is a great desire for religious freedom, and that we must expect a vigorous rebound after so much repression. But we should also ponder the fact that outside Poland the enthusiasms of faith and the weight of religious circles have not played a decisive role in recent uprisings, and that – whether as a result of compulsory de-Christianization or the universality of the process of secularization – this Europe is no more 'Christian' than the other. The precise information which comes to us from East Germany, to give just one example, is quite formal. And how will Poland itself develop after the return of complete religious freedom and a degree of economic improvement, when the Catholic church no longer has to play its role as guardian of the national and cultural identity of the country? It is not difficult to imagine . . .

So any contemporary enterprise of a spectacular 'new evangelization' seems doomed to failure. If it is based on the presupposition that there is a religious or Christian disposition towards a return of the past, its diagnosis is a mistaken one. And if it has taken the measure of the real newness which is called for, it is showing itself wrong about the means adopted, if these are the spiritual immediacy, biblical fundamentalism and authoritarian stand-points from which it begins.

In my view, the only serious basis for a presence of and support for the gospel in a Europe in the making derives from quite a different mentality. Far from reckoning on pessimism or a sweeping negative judgment on modernity – for example by stressing the failure of moral liberalism or by exploiting social faults – such a mentality recognizes and supports all that is positive, being content to accept it rather than to control it. Such a mentality loyally accepts the *de facto* secularization of institutions and culture (which does not imply the adoption of a pseudo-neutrality or a libertarian ideology). It loyally accepts the heritage of the Enlightenment: the value of reason, the construction of the state and, correlatively, the rights of the individual and of collectives, the confidence placed in democracy (though this does not mean one has to be blind to the diversity of ideological choices that can be made under the aegis of the Enlightenment).

Such a mentality participates without a second thought, i.e. without a proselytizing aim or predetermined conclusions, in the common research called for by the unresolved ethical, political and social problems which arise in our time (though that does not mean that the gospel is neutral in such matters). It seeks to be concerned to maintain the discreet stance of the witness, playing to the full the card of the personalization of human existence and of the faith, far removed from any nostalgia and all the techniques of mass pressure (though this does not mean that one accepts the individualism and the privatization of the religious).

If this happens, convinced Christians who make no totalitarian claims, churches ready to serve and to renounce their leadership, may make at least some contribution to the spiritual reconstruction of Europe. This is a contribution expected by others, but the new element is that it is not expected on just any conditions, and it may well also prove to be a presentation of the whole gospel, in its youth, its attraction and its freedom. Such a contribution to personal and public life is far removed from being a strategy. For to say 'Thy kingdom come' is not to look for a spectacular installation of 'Christ the King'. In keeping with the Incarnation, it is to hope that the kingdom of the Beatitudes will filter into this world quite gently, until it turns it upside down.[*]

Jean-Pierre Jossua

[*]I had already written these lines when I received the collected volume *Le rêve de Compostelle. Vers la restauration d'une Europe chrétienne?*, edited by Rene Lunerau (Paris, Centurion, 1989). This is a remarkable work, which sheds much light on many aspects of this discussion.

Translated by John Bowden

I · Historical Retrospect

The French Constitution

Decreed by the National Constituent Assembly in the years 1789,
1790 and 1791

Declaration of the Rights of Man and of the Citizen

The representatives of the French people, constituted in national assembly, considering ignorance, neglect or contempt of the rights of man to
be the only causes of public misfortune and the corruption of governments,
have resolved to lay down in a solemn declaration the natural, inviolable,
legitimate and sacred rights of man, so that this declaration, constantly
before all members of the social body, should remind them at all times of
their rights and their duties; so that the acts of the legislative power and
those of the executive power, which can always be compared with the aim
of any political institution, may be all the more respected, so that the
complaints of citizens, henceforth founded on simple and indisputable
principles, should always centre on the upholding of the constitution and
the common good. Consequently, the National Assembly declares and
recognizes, in the presence and under the auspices of the Supreme Being,
the following rights of man and the citizen:

I. Men are born and remain free and equal in rights. Social distinctions
can only be founded on general usefulness.

II. The aim of every political association is the preservation of the natural
and inviolable rights of man. These rights are liberty, property, safety and
resistance to oppression.

III. The principle of all sovereignty resides essentially in the nation. No
body, no individual can exercise authority which does not derive expressly
from it.

IV. Liberty consists of being able to do anything which is not harmful to
another person. Thus the exercise of the natural rights of every man is

limited only by the need to ensure that other members of society enjoy these same rights. These limits can only be determined by law.

V. The law only has the right to forbid actions harmful to society. Anything which is not forbidden by law cannot be prevented, and no one can be compelled to do what is not ordained by law.

VI. The law is the expression of general will. All citizens have the right to work, personally or through their religion, towards its establishment. It must be the same for everyone, whether it protects or punishes. All citizens, being equal in its eyes, are equally admissible to all offices, posts and public employment, according to their abilities, and with no other distinction but that of their virtues and talents.

VII. No man can be accused, arrested or detained except in cases determined by law and according to the forms which it has prescribed. Those who solicit, expedite, carry out or have carried out arbitrary orders must be punished; but any citizen legally arrested must obey immediately; any resistance makes him guilty.

VIII. The law should establish only strictly and obviously necessary penalties, and no one can be punished except by virtue of a law which has been established and promulgated before the offence, and legally applied.

IX. Every man being presumed innocent until he has been declared guilty, if it is considered essential to arrest him, any unnecessary force to secure his person should be severely repressed by law.

X. No one should be harrassed for his opinions, even religious opinions, provided that they do not disturb public order as established by law.

XI. Freedom of thought and expression is one of the most precious rights of man. Every citizen can therefore speak, write and print freely, subject to the responsibility for the abuse of such liberty in cases determined by law.

XII. A guarantee of the rights of man and of the citizen necessitates a public force. This force is therefore instituted for the advantage of all and not for the particular use of those to whom it is entrusted.

XIII. For the maintenance of the public force and its administrative expenses, a common tax is necessary. It should be shared equally among all citizens in proportion to their means.

XIV. All citizens have the right to ascertain, by themselves or through their representatives, the necessity of the public tax, to agree to it freely, to supervise its use and to determine its quota, its assessment, its payment and its duration.

XV. Society has the right to call to account any public agent of its administration.

XVI. Any society in which rights are not guaranteed and the division of powers is not laid down has no constitution.

XVII. Property being an inviolable and sacred right, no one can be deprived of it, except when public necessity, legally established, clearly demands it, on condition of a fair and previously agreed indemnity.

Universal Declaration of Human Rights

Adopted by the General Assembly, 10 December 1948

Preamble

Whereas recognition of the inherent dignity and of the equal and inalienable rights of all members of the human family is the foundation of freedom, justice and peace in the world,

Whereas disregard and contempt for human rights have resulted in barbarous acts which have outraged the conscience of mankind, and the advent of a world in which human beings shall enjoy freedom of speech and belief and freedom from fear and want has been proclaimed as the highest aspiration of the common people,

Whereas it is essential, if man is not to be compelled to have recourse, as a last resort, to rebellion against tyranny and oppression, that human rights should be protected by the rule of law,

Whereas it is essential to promote the development of friendly relations between nations,

Whereas the peoples of the United Nations have in the Charter reaffirmed their faith in fundamental human rights, in the dignity and worth of the human person and in the equal rights of men and women and have determined to promote social progress and better standards of life in larger freedom,

Whereas Member States have pledged themselves to achieve, in co-operation with the United Nations, the promotion of universal respect for and observance of human rights and fundamental freedoms,

Whereas a common understanding of these rights and freedoms is of the greatest importance for the full realization of this pledge.

Now, Therefore,

The General Assembly

proclaims

This universal declaration of human rights as a common standard of achievement for all peoples and all nations, to the end that every individual and every organ of society, keeping this Declaration constantly in mind, shall strive by teaching and education to promote respect for these rights and freedoms and by progressive measures, national and international, to secure their universal and effective recognition and observance, both among the peoples of Member States themselves and among the peoples of territories under their jurisdiction.

Article 1

All human beings are born free and equal in dignity and rights. They are endowed with reason and conscience and should act towards one another in a spirit of brotherhood.

Article 2

Everyone is entitled to all the rights and freedoms set forth in this Declaration, without distinction of any kind, such as race, colour, sex, language, religion, political or other opinion, national or social origin, property, birth or other status.

Furthermore, no distinction shall be made on the basis of the political, jurisdictional or international status of the country or territory to which a person belongs, whether it be independent, trust, non-self-governing or under any other limitation of sovereignty.

Article 3

Everyone has the right to life, liberty and security of person.

Article 4

No one shall be held in slavery or servitude; slavery and the slave trade shall be prohibited in all their forms.

Article 5

No one shall be subjected to torture or to cruel, inhuman or degrading treatment or punishment.

Article 6

Everyone has the right to recognition everywhere as a person before the law.

Article 7
All are equal before the law and are entitled without any discrimination to equal protection of the law. All are entitled to equal protection against any discrimination in violation of this Declaration and against any incitement to such discrimination.

Article 8
Everyone has the right to an effective remedy by the competent national tribunals for acts violating the fundamental rights granted him by the constitution or by law.

Article 9
No one shall be subjected to arbitrary arrest, detention or exile.

Article 10
Everyone is entitled in full equality to a fair and public hearing by an independent and impartial tribunal, in the determination of his rights and obligations and of any criminal charge against him.

Article 11
1. Everyone charged with a penal offence has the right to be presumed innocent until proved guilty according to law in a public trial at which he has had all the guarantees necessary for his defence.
2. No one shall be held guilty of any penal offence on account of any act or omission which did not constitute a penal offence, under national or international law, at the time when it was committed. Nor shall a heavier penalty be imposed than the one that was applicable at the time the penal offence was committed.

Article 12
No one shall be subjected to arbitrary interference with his privacy, family, home or correspondence, nor to attacks upon his honour and reputation. Everyone has the right to the protection of the law against such interference or attacks.

Article 13
1. Everyone has the right to freedom of movement and residence within the borders of each state.
2. Everyone has the right to leave any country, including his own, and to return to his country.

Article 14
1. Everyone has the right to seek and to enjoy in other countries asylum from persecution.

2. This right may not be invoked in the case of prosecutions genuinely arising from non-political crimes or from acts contrary to the purposes and principles of the United Nations.

Article 15
1. Everyone has the right to a nationality.
2. No one shall be arbitrarily deprived of his nationality nor denied the right to change his nationality.

Article 16
1. Men and women of full age, without any limitation due to race, nationality or religion, have the right to marry and to found a family. They are entitled to equal rights as to marriage, during marriage and at its dissolution.
2. Marriage shall be entered into only with the free and full consent of the intending spouses.
3. The family is the natural and fundamental group unit of society and is entitled to protection by society and the State.

Article 17
1. Everyone has the right to own property alone as well as in association with others.
2. No one shall be arbitrarily deprived of his property.

Article 18
Everyone has the right to freedom of thought, conscience and religion; this right includes freedom to change his religion or belief, and freedom, either alone or in community with others and in public or private, to manifest his religion or belief in teaching, practice, worship and observance.

Article 19
Everyone has the right to freedom of opinion and expression; this right includes freedom to hold opinions without interference and to seek, receive and impart information and ideas through any media and regardless of frontiers.

Article 20
1. Everyone has the right to freedom of peaceful assembly and association.
2. No one may be compelled to belong to an association.

Article 21
1. Everyone has the right to take part in the government of his country, directly or through freely chosen representatives.
2. Everyone has the right of equal access to public service in his country.

3. The will of the people shall be the basis of the authority of government; this will shall be expressed in periodic and genuine elections which shall be by universal and equal suffrage and shall be held by secret vote or by equivalent free voting procedures.

Article 22
Everyone, as a member of society, has the right to social security and is entitled to realization, through national effort and international co-operation and in accordance with the organization and resources of each State, of the economic, social and cultural rights indispensable for his dignity and the free development of his personality.

Article 23
1. Everyone has the right to work, to free choice of employment, to just and favourable conditions of work and to protection against unemployment.
2. Everyone, without any discrimination, has the right to equal pay for equal work.
3. Everyone who works has the right to just and favourable remuneration ensuring for himself and his family an existence worthy of human dignity, and supplemented, if necessary, by other means of social protection.
4. Everyone has the right to form and to join trade unions for the protection of his interests.

Article 24
Everyone has the right to rest and leisure, including reasonable limitation of working hours and periodic holidays with pay.

Article 25
1. Everyone has the right to a standard of living adequate for the health and well-being of himself and of his family, including food, clothing, housing and medical care and necessary social services, and the right to security in the event of unemployment, sickness, disability, widowhood, old age or other lack of livelihood in circumstances beyond his control.
2. Motherhood and childhood are entitled to special care and assistance. All children, whether born in or out of wedlock, shall enjoy the same social protection.

Article 26
1. Everyone has the right to education. Education shall be free, at least in the elementary and fundamental stages. Elementary education shall be compulsory. Technical and professional education shall be made generally

available and higher education shall be equally accessible to all on the basis of merit.

2. Education shall be directed to the full development of the human personality and to the strengthening of respect for human rights and fundamental freedoms. It shall promote understanding, tolerance and friendship among all nations, racial or religious groups, and shall further the activities of the United Nations for the maintenance of peace.

3. Parents have a prior right to choose the kind of education that shall be given to their children.

Article 27

1. Everyone has the right freely to participate in the cultural life of the community, to enjoy the arts and to share in scientific advancement and its benefits.

2. Everyone has the right to the protection of the moral and material interests resulting from any scientific, literary or artistic production of which he is the author.

Article 28

Everyone is entitled to a social and international order in which the rights and freedoms set forth in this Declaration can be fully realized.

Article 29

1. Everyone has duties to the community in which alone the free and full development of his personality is possible.

2. In the exercise of his rights and freedoms, everyone shall be subject only to such limitations as are determined by law solely for the purpose of securing due recognition and respect for the rights and freedoms of others and of meeting the just requirements of morality, public order and the general welfare in a democratic society.

3. These rights and freedoms may in no case be exercised contrary to the purposes and principles of the United Nations.

Article 30

Nothing in this Declaration may be interpreted as implying for any State, group or person any right to engage in any activity or to perform any act aimed at the destruction of any of the rights and freedoms set forth herein.

Human Rights: A Historical Overview

Leonard Swidler

A human right is a claim to be able and allowed to perform an action because one is a human being – not because one is a citizen, or is permitted in law, or has a grant from the king or the pope, or for any other reason. To claim a right simply on the basis that one is a human is already a revolutionary act. Just as revolutionary is the notion that what it means to be human is an unending developing process, which implies that those things which can be claimed as rights on the basis of one's humanity are not statically fixed. Because the human person is a historical being, and therefore changing, so too human rights are historical realities, and therefore changing.

The idea of human rights as we understand it today is something that has developed in Western civilization. It is not that no other civilization has been concerned with the human. Confucianism, for example, can be said to be a kind of humanism *par excellence*. But even there the human being had rights only insofar as he occupied a certain position in society. The person had rights not as a human being as such, but as a son, father, brother, or whatever. The idea of human rights, however, is based on the affirmation of a certain level of individualism wherein the individual person would be valued for her/his own sake, and not just as a relationship to others.

I. The pillars of Western civilization – and human rights

Though it is only in modern times that our notion of human rights has developed, it has its foundations in the two pillars of Western civilization: Judeo-Christian religion and Greco-Roman culture. Let us look briefly at the latter first.

Plato, Aristotle, the Stoics and others in Hellenistic civilization developed the notion of a natural law, under whose jurisdiction the human fell. It was the Greeks who created the ideal and reality of democracy, wherein the citizen had certain fundamental rights simply by being born into the society. Nevertheless, the Stoics, starting with their founder Zeno, like the Confucians, also thought of humanity in hierarchical orders – which appear in the New Testament as the (in)famous Household Codes in the deutero-Pauline and pseudo–Petrine letters. At the bottom of society were the slaves, then came children, then women and then free male adults.

Perhaps the greatest contribution of the Romans to Western civilization was the fantastic development of law. However, as they absorbed more alien peoples into their empire they did not apply their Roman civil law to them, but rather their own indigenous law as far as possible. (This differentiation also turns up in the New Testament when Paul, though a proud Jew, claims the right to be tried under Roman civil law because he is also a Roman citizen.) Nevertheless, the Romans found many fundamentals of law which applied across all nations, a *ius gentium*, or 'common law of all humans' (*commune omnium hominum ius*), as the third-century Roman jurist Gaius phrased it. Here indeed is a basis for claiming a right simply on the grounds of one's humanity, for at the foundation of all there lies nature, which can be discovered by reason – and only humans have that.

The second pillar of Western civilization, and the essential foundation of the idea of human rights, is the Judeo-Christian religion. It begins with the beginning of the Hebrew Bible, the story of creation. All ethnic groups have come up with their own creation stories, covering the largest imaginable range of possible explanations. What was special about the Hebrews' explanation of the origin of the world was their claim that everything came from one source. There were not many gods who were responsible for the various parts of the world about us, as the different kinds of polytheism explained. Rather, the Hebrews argued, there was just one Source, one God, of all reality, and all reality flowing from God was good; the source of evil in the world – and its presence was as obvious to the ancient Hebrews as it is to us – was humankind.

An important point to notice here is the claim that because there was only one Source of all reality, the order encoded into all reality would also be one, and that included humankind, God's crowning creation, God's 'image', *imago Dei*. Humans would live in paradise, a well-ordered 'garden of delight' (as 'Eden' means), if they would simply follow the instructions, the order, God had structured into their very being. That meant that all humans were to be treated with the same reverence and respect because they were all created by the one God, and God created them all good – at the end of each day of creation the Genesis story says, 'and God saw that it was good (*tov* in the Hebrew)', and at the end of the sixth day it says that 'God saw that it was very good' (*mod tov*) – and in God's image.

Unlike the other ancient nations, which were polytheistic and hence had one set of rules by which to treat their own people and another set for other peoples, the Hebrews were committed, at least in theory, to treating all human beings by the same ethical rules. This is the burden of the phrase 'ethical monotheism', which describes the unique place the Hebrew religion held among all the religions of the ancient world. Also crucial in the creation story is the description of humankind being created in the image of God – hence having infinite worth and dignity.

Here, then, are the two elements of the Judeo-Christian root source of the modern notion of human rights: ethical monotheism and the image of God.

II. Religious liberty

Because in the ancient world, and in many instances even into late modern times, the nation and its religion were largely congruent, the degree of religious liberty granted is an important touchstone of the advance of the notion of 'human' rights (thought not the only one). Also, because religion – which might be defined as 'an explanation of the ultimate meaning of life, and how to live accordingly' – is such a foundational element of a person's humanity, granting persons the right to practise their own religion approaches granting them that right on the grounds of their humanity. This again makes religious liberty an important bellwether of the notion of human rights.

In this context the Christian church started out gloriously, only to slide into the mire of power corruption. In the pre-Constantinian era Christian writers laid vigorous claim to religious liberty – and from the fiery pen of Tertullian even with the term 'human right':

> It is a fundamental human right, a privilege of nature, that all human beings should worship according to their own convictions; one human person's religion neither harms nor helps another. It is not proper to force religion. It must be undertaken freely, not under pressure.

In a way, a high point of religious liberty, and thus much of the basis of human rights, was reached publicly with the universal declaration for the whole Roman Empire in the Edict of Milan (AD 313) by the emperor Constantine: 'We should therefore give both to Christianity and to all others free facility to follow the religion which they may desire.' This moment of freedom was, however, short-lived, for in AD 380 the Edict of Thessalonica was issued by the emperor Theodosius, stating that, 'It is our will that all the peoples who are ruled by the administration of Our Clemency shall practise that religion which the divine Peter the Apostle transmitted to the Romans.'

Even that great theological light of the West, Augustine, wrote against following one's conscience, except when it was correct – and in religious/ethical matters Christianity of course had a monopoly on correctness. Fortunately that even greater theological light of the West, Thomas Aquinas, following his great teacher Albert the Great, argued in favour of always following one's conscience, even if the pope claimed that it was erroneous!

III. America's contribution

After the demise of the Western Roman Empire and the slow emergence of Western European civilization, the long struggle for human rights took a major step toward the modern reality in thirteenth-century England when the barons forced the power-hungry King John to grant them a series of rights written down in the *Magna Carta* (AD 1215). Although many specific rights were spelled out here, perhaps the most fundamental was that no punishment could be imposed without due process of law. Obviously here again human reason was the foundation stone, thereby providing a solid basis for the building of the full-blown idea of human rights.

The sixteenth-century Protestant Reformation – particularly in its so-called Radical wing – moved agonizingly in the direction of religious liberty, with the mainline Protestants eventually establishing religious liberty, though with some restrictions, in the Netherlands under William the Silent.

But it was most of all in the 'new world' that religious liberty developed. It appeared first in the 1632 Charter of Maryland, and the practice of the Catholic Cecil Calvert, the second Lord Baltimore, to whom the Charter was granted. In 1663 under the leadership of the Baptist Roger Williams the tiny colony of Rhode Island was formed with a charter including a guarantee of religious liberty – for all Protestants. This was followed by the 1677 'Concessions and Agreements of West New Jersey' (most probably written by the staunch Quaker and freedom-lover William Penn) which provided for total religious liberty. In 1682 when William Penn founded his own colony ('Penn's Woods', Pennsylvania, with its first settlement the 'City of Brotherly and Sisterly Love', Philadelphia) he of course included religious liberty in its 'Frame of Government', as well as many expanded democratic principles and practices.

Shortly thereafter events in the mother country, England, moved the cause of human rights forward. King James II became a Catholic and was perceived as a threat by many Protestant Englishmen. Consequently he was deposed in 1688 in the so-called 'Glorious Revolution', which brought William of Orange and his wife Mary of England to the throne on condition of granting the various rights listed in the 1689 'Bill of Rights'. Although it provided religious liberty only for Protestants, it was a very positive and influential model for subsequent American bills of rights.

It was also at this time that the English philosopher John Locke wrote his influential *Two Treatises on Government*, in which he spoke at length about the natural law (building particularly on the work of scholars like Grotius and Pufendorf), the separation of governmental powers (it was Montesquieu who later spoke of the three separate powers of government: executive, legislative and judicial), and the right of all to 'life, liberty and property'. They were in a way a philosophical justification of the 'Glorious Revolution' and 'Bill of Rights', and had a strong influence on subsequent American political developments, including the 1776 US Declaration of Independence with its paraphrase of Locke: 'All men are created equal . . . with certain unalienable rights . . . life, liberty and the pursuit of happiness.'

Human rights matters moved relatively gradually until the last quarter of the eighteenth century. In 1774 the First Continental Congress of the thirteen American colonies issued its 'Declaration and Resolves' in which for the first time the law of nature was explicitly made the foundation of rights: 'By the immutable laws of nature . . . the following RIGHTS . . . life, liberty and property . . .' Then came the fateful year of 1776, with its Declaration of Independence.

However, even before the Declaration of Independence, and formative of it, was the issuance of the Bill of Rights of the Constitution of Virginia on 12 June 1776. It was drafted largely by George Mason. Its words rang out:

All men are by nature equally free and independent, and have certain inherent rights, of which, when they enter into a state of society, they cannot by any compact, deprive or divest their posterity; namely, the enjoyment of life and liberty, with the means of acquiring and possessing property, and pursuing and obtaining happiness and safety . . . All power is vested in, and consequently derived from, the people.

Among the many human rights listed were complete religious liberty for all, choice of leaders, due process of law, and, for the first time in any document of constitutional import, freedom of the press. There quickly followed that same year constitutions or bills of rights of Pennsylvania, Delaware, Maryland and North Carolina, all largely patterned on the Virginia Bill of Rights, and, most importantly and influentially, the Declaration of Independence, drafted by Thomas Jefferson of Virginia.

After winning the War of Independence in 1781, the United States of America was governed by the Articles of Confederation, which proved inadequate, and so in 1787 a new Constitution was drafted and adopted. However, in the process of its acceptance by the various constituent states the appending of a Bill of Rights was demanded. One was consequently drafted by James Madison (also from Virginia) and submitted to Congress on 28 July 1789 – almost simultaneously with parallel events in France – and adopted later that year as the first ten amendments of the US Constitution, known as the American Bill of Rights – a succinct list of human rights as then understood.

Revolutionary events were also occurring in France in the latter part of the eighteenth century. Although many basic human rights were viciously violated in the quarter-century of turmoil and change that was unleashed with the storming of the Bastille on 14 July 1789, a landmark document in the history of human rights was forged almost at the very beginning of the French Revolution – the *Declaration des droits des hommes et citoyens*, a French, but now for the first time universalized, version of the Enlightenment's notion of human rights, passed on 27 August 1789.

The *Declaration* largely repeated the preceding American and English precedents, as is clear even from the language used. It

proclaims, in the presence and under the auspices of the Supreme Being, the following rights of man and the citizen. 1. Men are born and remain free and equal in rights . . . preservation of the natural and inalienable rights of man; these rights are liberty, property, security, and resistance to oppression. 3. The source of all sovereignty resides essentially in the nation. . . . Law is the expression of the general will. . . . No man may be accused, arrested, or detained except in the cases determined by law, and according to the forms prescribed thereby.

As the German historian Martin Göhring noted, 'It was not wholly without significance that the soldier of freedom, La Fayette, who had fought for the independence of America and had been present when the American declaration was proclaimed, was the first to propose a declaration of rights to the National Assembly.''[1]

IV. Nineteenth- and twentieth-century developments

Despite the glorious language used in these English, American and French human-rights documents of the seventeenth and eighteenth centuries, there were still manifold restrictions on who qualified as human. For example, non-property owners in America did not fully qualify until the second quarter of the nineteenth century and slaves not until the third quarter; women did not make it into the charmed circle of voters until the twentieth century. Further, the understanding not only of 'human' but also of 'right' underwent a constant evolution – and doubtless will continue to do so. The newly developed twentieth-century claim to the right to work (United Nations 1948 'Universal Declaration of Human Rights', Art. 23) is a good example:

> The development of this new control over nature – first over external nature and increasingly also over human nature . . . has made possible entirely new dimensions of human self-development, and its apparently illimitable expansion leads to the expectation, at least in the developed countries, that it can release a sufficient potential so that everyone can participate in them – and consequently has a right to participate therein.[2]

Various steps in the expansion of the idea and reality of human rights were taken throughout the nineteenth century and into the twentieth. A major opportunity at the end of World War I was, unfortunately, passed up. In 1919 the President of the United States, Woodrow Wilson, drafted the Covenant of the League of Nations in person, using his own typewriter, incorporating a number of human rights. One of Wilson's proposals was to include an article on religious liberty in the Covenant, but it was scuttled as soon as Japan sought to link it with racial equality and the equality of states. Thus, the League of Nations Covenant contained no mention of human rights, though in fact the League did protect a number of them through the 'Minority Protection Treaties'.

V. The UN and the Universal Declaration

The next milestone in the internationalizing of human rights was also set down by an American president, Franklin D. Roosevelt, when he delivered his famous address to Congress on 6 January 1941, on the Four Freedoms. In it he outlined the four essential freedoms upon which the whole world should be founded: freedom of speech and expression, freedom of religion, freedom from want, and freedom from fear:

> Roosevelt was explicit in stressing that these freedoms were to be secured everywhere in the world, that is to say, on a universal basis. He made it clear that traditional freedoms of speech and of worship should go hand in hand with such wider human rights as economic and social welfare and peace and security for all peoples and persons.[3]

It is rather striking how Roosevelt anticipated – and influenced? – the development of the so-called three generations of human rights: first generation, civil and political rights; second generation, social and economic rights; third generation, rights of world development and peace.

A year later, in January 1942, the Allied Powers spoke of human rights globally when they claimed that 'complete victory over their enemies is essential to defend life, liberty, independence and religious freedom and to preserve human rights and justice in their own lands as well as in other lands'.[4] These two statements provided an immediate vision for the framing of the United Nations Charter in San Francisco in 1945. Among the purposes of the UN, it stated, were: 'To achieve international cooperation . . . in promoting and encouraging respect for human rights and for fundamental freedoms for all without distinction as to race, sex, language or religion.'

One of the first acts of the UN General Assembly, in January 1946, was to recommend 'the formulation of an international Bill of Rights'. A year later the newly created UN Commission on Human Rights chose as its President Eleanor Roosevelt, and immediately set to work on drafting the 'Universal Declaration of Human Rights', which was adopted on 10 December 1948.

> It is noteworthy that one of those who played an important part in the formulation of the draft Universal Declaration of Human Rights was Monsignor Roncalli, as he then was, subsequently Pope John XXIII. Monsignor Roncalli was then Papal Nuncio in Paris . . . He often, in

conversations with me, expressed the hope that the Universal Declaration would save humanity from another war.

The eminent French jurist and Nobel Peace Laureate, the late René Cassin, has paid eloquent tribute to the assistance which Monsignor Roncalli then gave to the French Delegation. This may also possibly explain the fact that some fifteen years later in his Encyclical *Pacem in Terris*, Pope John XXIII lays specific reference on the need for a Charter of Fundamental Human Rights.[5]

For some eighteen years the UN struggled to translate the Universal Declaration into legally binding instruments, which together with the Declaration are known as 'The International Bill of Human Rights', namely, the 'International Covenant on Economic, Social and Cultural Rights', the 'International Covenant on Civil and Political Rights', and the 'Optional Protocol to the International Covenant on Civil and Political Rights' – all adopted in 1966. A number of countries have explicitly incorporated large elements of this 'Bill of Human Rights' into their own foundational legal documents, and by now it has come to have the force of law in international law (which, other than world opinion, unfortunately does not have an effective enforcing agency).

Many other declarations and conventions on specific dimensions of human rights have been issued since 1948 by the UN and also regional bodies, like the Council of Europe. Sadly, a spelled-out declaration on religious liberty did not, as expected, quickly follow the superb *Study of Discrimination in the Matters of Religious Rights and Practices* in 1959 by the UN Special Rapporteur Arcot Krishnaswami. It was only in 1981 that the 'Declaration on the Elimination of All Forms of Intolerance and of Discrimination Based on Religion or Belief' was passed by the UN General Assembly. Nevertheless, it is clear that progress in human rights is being made – slowly and painfully, and often with a wide breach between theory and practice.

VI. The Catholic Church and human rights

The foundation of the claim for human rights is human reason and freedom; they, along with animality, are what make humans human. The search for truth, 'which makes us free', is a legacy the Christian church has from its founder, the Jew Jesus. In very many ways the church was largely true to this legacy in the beginning, but also in very many ways, especially after Constantine, it became largely untrue to this legacy. This was increasingly so in the reaction of much of the Catholic hierarchy to the Protestant Reformation, and most particularly so in its reaction to the Enlightenment and the concomitant human rights movement. This is not the place to replay the dirge of Christian reaction. Let a few notes (because of space limitations, from the Catholic section alone) suffice as a reminder.

In 1832 Pope Gregory XVI described liberty of conscience as the 'false and absurd, or rather mad principle (*deliramentum*), that we must secure and guarantee to each one liberty of conscience; this is one of the most contagious of errors . . . To this is attached liberty of the press, the most dangerous liberty, an execrable liberty, which can never inspire sufficient horror.' His successor from 1846 until 1878, Pius IX, did not hesitate to repeat that massive condemnation at least twice and make it his own. Even as late as the 1950s the American Jesuit John Courtney Murray was silenced by Rome for arguing that there was another, more faithful, line in Catholic tradition.

It is interesting to compare in this regard the language of Gregory and Pius (it is difficult to imagine how it could have been made more *ex cathedra*, and hence presumably 'infallible') with that of Pope John XXIII's *Pacem in terris*: 'Man has a natural right . . . to freedom of speech and publication . . . to worship God in accordance with the right dictates of his own conscience and to profess his religion in both private and public'; and of Vatican II's 'Declaration on Religious Liberty':

> Man is bound to follow his conscience faithfully . . . he must not be forced to act contrary to his conscience. Nor must he be prevented from acting according to his conscience, especially in religious matters . . . Religious freedom in society is in complete harmony with the act of Christian faith.

It is both in the person of John XXIII and in the Second Vatican Council which he called into existence that we finally find the official Catholic breakthrough to religious freedom – and human rights in general. For over a century and a half the papacy fought bitterly against the Enlightenment and human rights movement, but with *Pacem in terris* in April 1963, issued only a few weeks before John XXIII's death, the papacy embraced the idea of human rights. John spoke with high praise of the United Nations and stated that 'a clear proof of the far-sightedness of this organization is provided by the Universal Declaration of Rights', which, as we heard above, he helped shape in 1947/8.

The theme of human rights turns up once again in a papal document with great positive stress in the first encyclical of Pope John-Paul II, *Redemptor hominis*, where among a welter of detail the pope writes:

We cannot fail to recall at this point, with esteem and profound hope for the future, the magnificent effort made to give life to the United Nations Organization, an effort conducive to the definition and establishment of man's objective and inviolable rights . . . There is no need for the Church to confirm how closely this problem is linked with her mission in the modern world. Indeed it is at the very basis of social and international peace, as has been declared by John XXIII . . .

Unfortunately much of the credibility of John Paul II's frequent preaching of strong pro-human rights in the secular sphere is severely undercut by his anti-human rights practice in the church sphere. This double standard, among other things, called into existence in 1979/80 – a period of severe papal repression – organizations like Christenrechte in der Kirche, Comité de défense des droits des chrétiens and Association for the Rights of Catholics in the Church – the latter produced a 'Charter of the Rights of Catholics in the *Church*', extending the work of the Universal Declaration of Human Rights into the Catholic Church.[6]

Notes

1. Martin Göhring, *Weg und Sieg der modernen Staatsidee in Frankreich*, Tübingen: Mohr-Siebeck 1946, p. 280.
2. Johannes Schwartländer (ed.), *Modernes Freiheitsethos und christlicher Glaube*, Munich: Kaiser; Mainz: Grünwald 1981, p. 11.
3. Theo C. van Boven, 'Religious Liberty in the Context of Human Rights', *The Ecumenical Review* 37 (July 1985), p. 347.
4. Sean MacBride (Nobel and Lenin Peace Laureate and recipient of the American Medal of Justice, and former Minister of Foreign Affairs, Ireland), 'The Universal Declaration – 30 Years After', in Alan D. Falconer (ed.), *Understanding Human Rights: An Interdisciplinary and Interfaith Study*, Dublin: Irish School of Ecumenics 1980, pp. 8f.
5. Ibid., p. 9.
6. See Leonard Swidler and Herbert O'Brien (eds.), *A Catholic Bill of Rights*, Kansas City, MO: Sheed & Ward 1988.

II · The Challenge of Human Rights to World Religions

The Torah, Written and Oral, and Human Rights: Foundations and Deficiencies

Eugene B. Borowitz

I. The one God and the dignity of the human person

The modern idea of human 'rights' does not exist in that conceptualization in classic Jewish doctrine, for neither the Bible nor rabbinic literature speaks of human dignity in this way. It is not difficult to understand why this is the case. The contemporary notion of human rights arose in connection with strong assertion of property rights; one has such significant entitlement to the property one has legally acquired that government exists in large part to safeguard one's claims in this regard. Jewish tradition over the millennia had great respect for property rights, yet it had even greater regard for God's ultimate possession of everything in creation. Theologically, the Jewish equivalent of 'rights' derives from the compelling Jewish response to God as the absolute 'owner' (*baal*, *koneh*), in the economic metaphor, or 'king' (*melekh*) in the related political usage, or more directly as 'creator' (*bore'*, *yotzer*). And it is not difficult to see these notions carried forward in the European euphemisms for God's own, ineffable name, the tetragrammaton, as in the English 'Lord'.

This affirmation of God's 'right' to everything must be associated with the equally strong Hebrew spiritual sensibility that God is one, alone, unique, the Entity incomparably greater than all those non-entities people call 'god'. Hence there is almost a hint of blasphemy in the assertion that individuals might have property or even personal rights that could in any way be like God's or, more heretically, allow one to challenge God's absolute status. (Modern writers have made much of the uncommon tales in biblical and later writings which depict God's worthies directly challenging God. However, they confront God only in terms of the 'rights' God has given them as God's covenant partners, not on the basis of some standard independent of people and God.)

Because this absolutely single God is good and in that goodness creates and relates to human beings, all of them, they have the Jewish equivalent of human rights. I wish to explicate here the theological foundations of this development; for a detailed examination of the parallels in Jewish law to many provisions of the United Nations' Universal Declaration of Human Rights, see the admirable work by Haim Cohn, *Human Rights in Jewish Law* (New York: KTAV Publishing House 1984).

To begin with, Judaism asserts that an inalienable dignity inheres in every human being and it may perhaps best be understood as a function of two closely related religious themes. The one is the astonishing assertion that God created human beings in God's own 'image'. Regardless of our exegesis of that richly ambiguous term, there is something about every human being which is identified with the absolute source of value in the universe. An even more daring belief, God's incomparable greatness and goodness being kept in mind, is the central Hebrew religious perception that God had brought humankind into active partnership with God, the relationship symbolized by the ancient Semitic legal term 'covenant'. As it were, humans are sufficiently godlike that God can be intimately involved with them, concerned about their behaviour and dedicated to their welfare. Their incomparable status among created things stems from this close identification with God and God's purposes.

II. Responsibility, justice, grace and the dignity of the human person

Perhaps no other concept of Jewish faith makes this more evident than does its notion of *teshuvah*, the turning back to God which English somewhat lamely terms 'repentance'. Being a covenant partner of God's involves each human being in precious responsibility; one is not only commanded by God but is then free to respond in obedience or defiance. Judaism thus understands God as endowing people with the freedom to turn against the very source of their supreme worth and status, thus bestowing on them an extraordinary intrinsic value. But should they exercise this freedom to defy God, to sin, this might conceivably result in their permanent estrangement from God and thus a loss of all human dignity. To some extent this aura attends the sinner.

Since God is central to traditional Judaism, the wicked, particularly those who self-consciously and defiantly transgress, are loathed – but they never lose their covenant partnership with God, even in just punishment. We see that most clearly in Judaism's proclamation of the ability of even hardened sinners to turn from their evil ways and 'live'. To Jonah's discomfiture, that is what happens when the vicious Ninevites give up their immorality and throw themselves on God's mercy, which is instantly granted. And rabbinic literature, in law and lore down to the present day, reaffirms this understanding of God's relationship with all humans as individuals and in their collectivities. In sum, Judaism teaches that no one can ever take away from a human being an elemental value which God has bestowed upon everyone and which God never alienates.

This motif is related to the strong emphases on justice and mercy in Jewish doctrine. That all are equal before human courts as they are before the divine judge, that the rich must receive no special deference and so too the poor are only legal equals, no more but no less, testifies to the inherent worth of each person. But the prophets and sages who shaped Jewish religious life are too sensitive to what God demands and what social realities make of human relationships to think that good statutes and legal procedures alone can produce God's sanctified community. They regularly enjoin us to be merciful as God is merciful to us, giving one another much more than what others might claim by right or we might think to grant them to gain some advantage. Each person symbolizes God and thus ought receive a precious measure of our love and concern.

Positively, this produces an expectation that people will be given the opportunity to develop their humanity through security of person, respect for privacy and reputation, encouragement of education and leisure, the chance to work and be compensated, to acquire property, to marry and found a family, and much else. All this is so fundamental to Judaism that it rarely reaches direct statement in the Bible or the Talmud. Rather, it is simply taken for granted by our sacred texts as the ground of all those many provisions of Jewish law and teaching which specify the details of existence made holy. That these many documents, written over centuries in different social circumstances, have so little need to explain or rationalize their fundamental world-view testifies to its enduring power in Jewish religiosity.

To a considerable extent, however, it is the negative aspects of the human situation that most tellingly indicate whether one has rights. Human relations are substantially ordered by the interplay power, which means that some people are often able to deny others their self-determination. In such situations of coercion the person with inferior power has little or no defence against the more powerful unless the victim has something like rights to fall back upon and, the realities of power being what they are, some countervailing power that can be called upon to enforce them. The analysis of one such situation, an important one for universal human rights, should clarify what is involved.

III. The treatment of outsiders – a test case

Even today in democracies with well-articulated notions of pluralism, aliens often find themselves discriminated against. In ancient times when the individual and the group were not differentiated as sharply as they are today, outsiders would normally expect to be treated with a strong suspicion or outright hatred. Indeed, we often consider it a critical test of one's ethics to see how one treats the outsider, how different are the standards one applies to members of one's own group and to those outside it. On this score the oldest Jewish sources are admirable. The Bible does not begin its account of human history with the origin of the Hebrews. Instead, it speaks first of God's relationship with humanity as a whole and specifically indicates how this comes to include all the 'tongues and nations' into which people have become divided. Two important lines of development proceed from this biblical understanding.

In the Talmud and thence through the rest of the development of Jewish law, the covenant God made with Noah and his children becomes the foundation of the Jewish theology of the Gentile, the non-Jew, and the many laws regarding Jewish–Gentile relations. Structurally, the Gentile relationship with God is the same as that between God and the Jewish people, namely, it is a covenant. God gives seven grounding commandments to all humankind: the prohibitions of idolatry, blasphemy, murder, theft, sexual immorality and eating a limb severed from a living animal, as well as the positive injunction to establish courts of justice.

Without much imaginative speculation one can infer from these duties the sense of human dignity to which they give social and religious form. Even more to the point, Jewish law substantially equates Jews and Noahides by two presumptions: first, that before the revelation at Mt Sinai Jews were obligated to serve God in exactly the same way as were Gentiles, and second, that after the giving of the Torah, the special revelation to the Jews, there was nothing prohibited to a Gentile that was now permitted to Jews. Of course, the judgment of the biblical authors and the rabbis that the Gentile nations all violated their covenant by their idolatry rendered them utterly wicked and reprobate in Jewish eyes. The critical point is that they were not condemned merely because they were Gentiles, religiously alien, but because of their behaviour. Thus, rabbinic tradition came to the authoritative position that pious individuals among the Gentiles, like Jews, had 'a share in the life of the world to come'. Clearly, the beliefs which ground this point of view could in a later age, one of much greater human interaction and equality, make possible a Jewish ground for a universal declaration of human rights.

A similar attitude toward the alien is found as a major motif in the Torah's legislation regarding the stranger who comes to live among Jews settled on their promised land. Empathically the law states that 'you must not oppress the stranger, for you know the heart of the strangers having yourselves been strangers in the land of Egypt' (Ex. 23.9). Or again: 'The stranger who resides with you shall be to you as one of the homeborn. You shall love him as yourself, for you were strangers in the land of Egypt. I am the Lord, your God' (Lev. 19.33). God is even described as telling the people of Israel, when reminding them that the land that they have been given remains God's, that 'you are but strangers, sojourning with me' (Lev. 25.23).

This theme requires greater emphasis, for it is not the stranger alone who is powerless in most societies. The Torah often calls upon the Hebrews to be particularly concerned about the widow and the orphan as well as the stranger. These three symbolize all those likely to be taken advantage of by the shrewd and the mighty, and it is just these that are described as God's special concern. Again and again the refrain sounded above, 'I am the Lord', is the only 'reason' given for this decency toward people one could easily outmanoeuvre. So too, one must not curse the deaf, though the words cannot be heard, or put a stumbling-block before the blind, though they will not know who did them harm, for 'I am the Lord'. God is their advocate and the power behind them, though society considers them insignificant and God will execute judgment on their behalf, in this life and, if not here, then in the life of the world to come. Eschatology as well as this-worldly retribution gives the powerless and thus all people a Vindicator, and one infringes upon the worth God has conferred upon them only with great personal risk.

In much of Jewish history these teachings did not have the universal scope and democratic aura they have today. For centuries Jewish belief and the Jewish people lived under continual threat, for the few Jewish monotheists existed as a most peculiar people in a world of often hostile idolaters. And later, when Christianity and Islam made belief in one God the common faith of the Western world, discrimination and hostility toward Jews made it realistic to maintain a limited Jewish ethical horizon. That their spiritual forebears living in such straitened circumstances had so fundamentally universal an appreciation of humankind seems to Jews today an awesome, numinous accomplishment. Then, when social circumstance changed and persecution gave way to equality, it was not difficult for Jewish thinkers searching their sacred tradition to recover and apply the old Jewish appreciation of human solidarity and inalienable individual human dignity.

IV. Problems of religious foundation

1. Religions of revelation versus the absoluteness of rights

As often, the problems connected with this religious understanding stem from its very strength. I do not see that these problems arise directly from the specific Jewish character of the faith outlined above. Rather I believe that they come from the difficulties created by modern, that is, Western thought for the discussion of religions based on revelation. One problem derives from the absolute character of the vision of humanity elaborated. Were the one, incomparable God not the source of universal human dignity, then in certain circumstances that dignity might be compromised or qualified. What gives the term 'rights' its high practical significance is precisely its unconditional character. In the face of overbearing power one can assert one's 'rights' and thus, ideally, prevent the would-be oppressors from doing their coercive will. When such rights exist, any effort to justify the imposition of the other's will by seeking to qualify the rights or make them conditional can be quickly identified as immoral and discriminatory. In this context, the absoluteness of rights is commendable.

We are troubled, however, because some religionists claim to know in detail the will of the One, absolute source of value in the universe. Anyone claiming a different or, worse, an opposite position, is then not only absolutely wrong but can be seen as an enemy of God and truth, and possibly in danger of damnation or its equivalent. It is but a step from this to what some rabbinic texts, in another context, term saving a sinner's soul at the cost of taking his life. That is, to be sure, an extreme case, but it is sufficiently exemplified in the history of religion world-wide, even into our own day, that it cannot be ignored. Religions of revelation – and even others which have no such concept – have, by their absolutism, occasionally generated extremism, zealotry and fanaticism. Thus there is a fearsome contradiction in advocating a religious position which can motivate denying others their rights as the foundation of a robust commitment to broad-scale human rights.

2. Universalism and particularism

The other major conundrum lies in the paradox that religions of revelation affirm the universal value of all human beings on a quite particularistic ground. That is, everything they have to say about humankind generally comes from their institutional version of what God has said, making the particularity as critical as the universalism. Thus though the Jewish tradition accords Gentiles the fullest human value as a result of the covenant made with Noah, how Gentiles know their status is critical to Jewish law. If they assert their Noahide status as a matter of their own reason, they forfeit their dignity in a Jewish jurisdiction where they must formally accept it as a matter of Jewish revelation or reap the consequences (Maimonides, *The Laws of Kings*, 8.10–11). This stipulation, which clashes with modern views of tolerance, has a religious logic to it. When revelation is the basis of all truth, to suggest that one might reach ultimate truth by another means is to challenge the premise of all premises. Hence the paradox that to benefit fully from the universal reach of the Jewish tradition, the Gentile must accept it in its particularity at least in part.

This seemed like an egregious case of ethnocentrism in the heady days when philosophers had no difficulty asserting as a matter of simple rationality that their ideas were characteristic of all human rationality. In that context the reference to a special level of human experience – particularly one limited to certain specific persons at some particular time – was adjudged a rather primitive level of thought. Modern secularity claimed to reach beyond such limited horizons of thought to a true universalism and claimed that it was ethically superior to Western religions as a consequence. In that time religion seemed more a hindrance to universal human rights than their needed foundation.

3. Eurocentrism

Only we no longer live in such self-confident secularity. What once passed for a broad universalism now seems quite particularistic, even Eurocentric, in the language of some critics. Others easily fault it as the guild product of a certain group of university professors, ones largely male, white and either Christian or highly influenced by Christian culture. Today few rationalists can confidently claim to stand above all the particularities of individual existence and speak in some compelling way of what everyone is or ought to be or needs or experiences or deserves – and thus the various rationalisms are no longer able to give a convincing rationale for the existence of universal human rights or the rational necessity to make them an operative reality in our world. Religion, for so long the beneficiary of the ethical chiding of secularists who pointed to its moral nakedness, is now able to return the compliment. How paltry a notion of human reason is the one our intellectuals have come to accept, one so impoverished that it cannot easily contain a substantive, commanding ethics! How shallow a sense of what it is to be human suffuses our culture, so that our artists and literati rarely venture beyond criticism to assert something positively and unqualifiedly about universal moral responsibility! In its confident advance beyond its revelatory ground, Western secularity lost its deep human bearings with ugly consequences now seen everywhere around us.

4. The role of one's own religion

With contemporary secularity in so sorry a human state, if human rights are to have a sure ground, it must now come from those religions, like Judaism, whose traditions provide ample grounds for affirming them. But that returns us to the problems of the absoluteness and the particularity of such religions. In Judaism, as in some other faiths, a response to these problems has been widely accepted, if rarely articulated. It rests on what may be called with some exaggeration a theological rejection of the logical law of the excluded middle. Either, so the old standards of proper reasoning held, a notion is absolute or it is relative; it is universal or it is particular. These stringent alternatives seem unreasonable to the modern Jewish religious sensibility. Yes, our faith is sufficiently sure and certain that we stake our lives and that of our community on it – and will do so until the messianic fulfilment arrives. But though we know our religious truth to be utterly decisive for us, we acknowledge our human limits in the religious realm. We do not also assert that we have the whole truth or the only truth about God and humankind. Others we have come to know have what we can recognize as their own truths. Not only must we in due humility give them the freedom to express and refine their truth, often we can learn from them while nonetheless seeing our own faith as decisive correct.

5. The actual contribution of Judaism

Something similar must be said about our particularity. Yes, it is our particular Jewish tradition which gives such power to our affirmation of universal human rights. If our people's God were not the good, concerned, unique Divinity we know our God to be, where would we gain the compelling insight that humankind in all its individual and corporate diversity and moral disability was nonetheless inalienably endowed with ultimate worth? And if we had not made our slavery in Egypt and our exodus thence to freedom a central human truth in our lives, one we have profoundly renewed as we have seen our people granted equality after centuries of degradation and persecution, would we be as dedicated as we are to extending human rights to every creature? Yet this truth we so centrally proclaim as part of our living faith is not exclusive to our people either as religious insight or human experience. Many others, in their own ways, have come to believe what we believe. We are not then surprised when they see in our old Exodus tale their deepest spiritual insight, for we know our particular religious vision also to be profoundly and indivisibly universal.

These sentiments are most easily expressed in the various liberal forms of Judaism. These movements, which emphasize the human partnership with God in the evolution of our faith, can see in our recent experience with democracy and pluralism an ethical instruction that we know must be part of our Judaism. Simply put, God has spoken to us in the experience of these two centuries since our emancipation from the ghetto began and we have learned, not the least because of our experience with the Holocaust, the ultimate value of universal human rights.

A large part of our Orthodox community has, in ways befitting its elemental dedication to the Written and Oral Torah as revealed by God to our people, found the notions of democracy and pluralism, so closely linked with that of universal human rights, congenial to their Judaism. For a religion as closely tied to human history as is ours, it is quite natural to take an almost pragmatic approach to the application of God's ultimate truth to given social circumstances. Perhaps the evident human gains which have come from getting people to live with one another in mutual respect will similarly one day affect the rest of our religious community and those other religious groups who have been reluctant to embrace even an unimperialistic universalism.

Gospel, Church Law and Human Rights: Foundations and Deficiencies

Knut Walf

I. Difficult beginnings

It is in the ancient pre- and extra-Christian philosophies of Greek and Greco-Roman provenance that we find the roots or beginnings of human rights in Western thinking. Generally speaking these philosophies place more stress upon the value of the individual than upon the social values. In Germanic and Slav societies, in the East Asiatic cultures, and evidently also in early American societies[1] the emphasis was placed rather upon the social dimensions of human rights. These different modes of evaluation have reached down to our own day – not only in human rights discussions between capitalist and socialist countries[2] but also in dialogues between representatives of Western and Eastern religions concerning the status of human rights.

In the gospel, the accent is chiefly and expressly social (in I Cor. 12.13 and Gal. 3.28); in contrast, statements about the dignity of the individual can be distilled only indirectly, e.g. by way of the dignity of Jesus Christ as being in the likeness of God (II Cor. 4.4; Col 1.15). Westermann has stated that the question of human rights can also be put to the Old Testament, though only in an indirect fashion. The social legislation which we find in the Old Testament also alludes to respect for values which we today count among human rights, e.g. opposition to discrimination against individual and particular groups such as slaves or foreigners.

The right to freedom of religion is, not, however, found anywhere in the Old Testament as a formal right.[3] Christian theologians have indeed asserted that 'both the concept and the reality of human rights are absolutely unknown in the Bible'.[4] Taking these findings as a whole, they represent an unclear and uncertain basis for the establishment of human rights. This situation has certainly exercised an influence upon the hesitating or even negative attitude of the Christian churches – an attitude which lasted into the twentieth century. This attitude has especially characterized the reaction of the Catholic Church to the question of human rights.

The general social conditions in Europe up to the Reformation did not permit any church opposition to develop against the blatant and widespread violations of basic rights as reflected, for instance, in the earlier social position of women or in the universal use of torture in the prosecution of the law. The church of course shared responsibility for these social conditions, though it is not easy to mete out today's judgments upon the transactions of those times. At the same time Luther did draw a distinction between 'rough human rights', 'rights of reason' and 'rights of faith and the gospel'.[5] The central insight of the Reformation into man's justification before God made all the churches of the Reformation acutely sensitive to individual responsibility, and, following from this, to the rights of the individual. The religious wars in the wake of the Reformation also contributed a great deal towards the recognition of the importance of corporate freedom of religion and, to a lesser degree, of individual freedom of conscience as well.

Human rights in the modern Euro-American sense were first formulated in Anglo-Saxon law. This is perhaps the reason why these values were more closely linked to the gospel than they were in Christian and later Catholic church law, where their roots reached deep into Roman law and were partly bound up with Hellenistic thinking. The aversion of Catholic church authorities to these formulated human rights can be traced back primarily to the expressly anti-Catholic (and anti-absolutist) orientation of the English Bill of Rights of 1689. The North American Bill of Rights, too, was pervaded by Protestant Bible piety, behind which, however, stood the deep seriousness of Christian feeling and attitudes along with morally upright as well as legal thinking.

It cannot, however, be denied that Protestant theology up into the twentieth century also maintained an aloof attitude to human rights. Protestant theology also displayed a negative attitude towards the values and achievements of the Western Enlightenment and of the modern European revolutions similar or even identical to that in the Catholic Church. In the final analysis, seemingly unbridgeable anthropologies long stood in the way of a positive evaluation of human rights by Christian theologians: on the part of the representatives of the Enlightenment a basically optimistic picture of man seen as ever capable of improvement;

on the Christian side, the doctrine of sinful, fallen mankind. These are diametrically different images of man. Only with the greatest difficulty could bridges of mutual understanding be built between them.

It was not, however, until the Declaration of Human Rights by the French National Assembly that the *Magisterium* of the Catholic Church saw itself provoked into taking up a position. Pope Pius VI (1775–1799) condemned the Declaration at first internally in an Address to the Consistory of Cardinals and then in 1791, after an almost two-year tactical delay, publicly as well: first in a Brief of 10 March which was levelled at the French 'Civil Constitution of the Clergy', and then, a little later, on 13 April 1791, in the Brief *Caritas* which was expressly devoted to this question. The papal document stated that the formulations of human rights on freedom of religion and freedom of the press were as contradictory to the principles of the church as the Declaration on the Equality of all Men. According to Pius VI, the principles of freedom and equality were being used entirely for the annihilation of the Catholic Church.

Up till the middle of the twentieth century the Christian churches as a whole experienced great difficulties in coming to acknowledge human rights. Since these rights had been proclaimed by the advocates of the anti-church French Revolution and in the nineteenth century had also become a non-negotiable component of all democratic movements, for varied, though interrelated, reasons the churches stood in the forefront of reactionary opposition. The Catholic Church viewed these ideas as a 'doctrine of unbridled freedom',[6] while the Protestant churches opposed them more by reason of these churches' intimate involvement with the authoritarian state than on theological grounds. It is nonetheless beyond dispute that even in the nineteenth century most constitutions or constitutional projects of the European countries possessed either an overall or a partial catalogue of basic and human rights.

II. Catholic church law

The 1983 *Code of Canon Law (Codex Iuris Canomici)* contains a catalogue of 'Obligations and Rights [the order is instructive] of all the Christian Faithful' (cc.208–223). The introductory c.208 speaks of 'a true equality' 'among all the Christian faithful'. The Code bases this upon a statement of the Second Vatican Council's *Dogmatic Constitution on the Church* (32, 3). This Council emphasized the dignity of the human person in another place as well (*The Declaration on Human Freedom*, 1, 1).

In interpreting these statements, however, Catholic authors often stress a distinction between basic church rights and universal human rights. They argue that basic church rights cannot be asserted in relation to the church whereas, on the other hand, human rights do exist in relation to the state. In the latter case, these rights are given to persons prior to and independently of the state whereas, in the former, rights 'are not given to Christians prior to and independently of the church. Basic church rights are, therefore, founded in the church itself'.[7] This very statement clearly shows the fundamental distinctions that still exist in the evaluation of human rights inside and outside the church. On the one hand, the Catholic Church compares itself with the state (cf. c.204 §2),[8] and on the other hand, it brings out differences between it and the state which limit the validity of and respect for human rights within the church. It is precisely this claim, by no means of recent origin, which has led, in the history of the church, to untold violations of human rights.

1. Universal basic church rights

Canons 212–220 of the new Code of Canon Law name the following rights: the right to free expression of opinion, freedom to form associations and freedom of assembly, freedom of inquiry and freedom of publication, the free choice of a state in life, the preservation of one's good name and one's privacy and the protection of the law. Canons 212 and 223 are especially important. Canon 212 §1 names the two pillars upon which the church community is established: the consciousness of the individual responsibility of the faithful in questions of faith and of obedience in these same questions to church leadership. In addition, c.212 §2, 3 guarantees a kind of right of objection on the part of the faithful towards measures of the church authorities. The language of the canon, it is true, reveals that the legislator is still fixed in the mentality of the age of feudalism since this right is made dependent upon knowledge, competence and pre-eminence. Further, the faithful may make their opinion known only 'with due regard for the integrity of faith and morals and reverence towards their pastors, and with consideration for the common good and the dignity of persons'. In c.223 §2, finally, we meet with a general phrase, which is not the kind a jurist likes to see, according to which it is for the church authorities to regulate the exercise of these basic rights. The church authorities can, therefore, interpret and even narrow down at their own discretion the catalogue of basic rights, which are in any case restricted.

Now we cannot comment on these basic church rights, this welcome novelty in church law, without also looking into other areas of the new

Code, far less in isolation from the everyday reality of the church. Here the problems begin. I shall illustrate this with some examples.

The principle of equality (c.208) stands at the beginning of the catalogue of basic rights in the new Code of Canon Law. This canon may not be understood, however, in the sense of equality of rights of woman and man in the Catholic Church. Pope John XXIII spoke out for human rights in his encyclical *Pacem in Terris* (1963). In this he also acknowledged that women rightly demand 'both in domestic and in public life the rights and duties which belong to them as human persons'.[9]

Let us go on to consider the basic right of political conviction. In contrast to the earlier 1917 Code, the new Code of Canon Law contains some stipulations which oblige clergy as well as laity in the service of the church to abstain from politics. According to c.317 §4, for example, those faithful 'who exercise leadership in political parties' may not be in positions of leadership in public church associations.[10] The new Code strictly forbids clergy to have an active role in political parties and in the direction of trade unions 'unless the need to protect the rights of the Church or to promote the common good requires it in the judgment of the competent ecclesiastical authority' (c.287 §2). There are even stricter prohibitions in the laws of particular churches, e.g. in the Federal Republic of Germany where the 'Declaration of the German Bishops on the Party-political Activity of Priests' of September 1973 prohibited not only priests but anyone involved in church services from engaging in political activity.[11]

2. *Freedom of opinion*

On the basic right of freedom of opinion, the Second Vatican Council took up a position which was new for the Catholic Church. In the Pastoral Constitution on the Church in the Modern World the right to freedom of assembly, of association and of opinion was evaluated positively, though admittedly in general terms and in reference to the state.[12]

However, this text also envisaged consequences within the life of the church. The Pastoral Constitution (62, 6) also contains the following important statement: 'In order that such persons may fulfil their proper function [viz. theological inquiry and teaching], let it be recognized that all the faithful, clerical and lay, possess a lawful freedom of inquiry and of thought, and the freedom to express their minds humbly and courageously about those matters in which they enjoy competence.' In the light of this statement, today's climate of the intimidation and disciplining of theologians and laity by the church authorities seems like a different programme altogether. It is common knowledge, however, that today's situation is in no way unique. There were many comparable periods in church history when the suppression of freedom of opinion was the normal state of affairs. There were reasons for this.

The opponents of freedom of opinion in the church often combine this concept with the 'freedom of belief' which the catalogues of universal human rights or basic human rights also indeed guarantee.[13] Wolfgang Rüfner, the German expert on state-church law, writes: 'Full freedom of opinion and of faith cannot, however, be transferred to the church as a faith community. It can only be a matter of providing the community with more elbow-room.'[14] The mistake in this thinking about freedom of opinion and its validity in the inner-church domain begins with the linking of the two concepts, freedom of opinion and freedom of faith. In the universal catalogues of basic rights, on the other hand, both are rightly guaranteed in strict separation from each other.

Each of the two freedoms has its own validity, different from the others. Freedom of faith is a part of freedom of religion and, indeed, of individual freedom of religion which we need to distinguish from corporate freedom of religion. Within a faith-community, individual freedom of religion, the freedom of faith, finds its external limits which will need to be observed. Their constant infringement must ultimately involve the consequence of separation or expulsion from the faith community. That freedom of thought and conscience remains unaffected by this was acknowledged by the Second Vatican Council – obviously against the opposition of the conservative minority. A special investigation would be necessary to determine how far Canon Law – including the 1983 Code – takes account of these facts.

Catholic law is 'spiritual law' which not only regulates the so-called external domain (*forum externum*) but also lays claim to control over the internal domain (*forum internum*). This, it is true, is not identical with the sphere of conscience. However the boundaries within the sphere of convictions and opinions are fluid and therefore unclear. It is from this situation that the disciplinary measures of the church's supervisory authorities originate and are legitimated.

III. Deficiencies in church law

Anyone who has ever had anything to do with church administration or indeed with church courts knows how great the reluctance is to apply the norms of church law. This is so particularly in the area of administration. Out of a misconceived regard for those involved there is preference for agreements which are not legally binding and are not verifiable. Objections to acts of church administration, especially those of the episcopal authorities, still seen far from materializing, so for this reason alone an uncertainty about the law prevails in the Catholic Church which is quite unbelievable to those outside it. Apart from the lack of an administrative court procedure, this uncertainty derives ultimately from one main cause, namely, the theologically plausible but legally increasingly more questionable unity of powers in the Catholic Church.

1. Unity or separation of powers

The Viennese canon lawyer Erwin Melichar dealt in detail with this question in his 1948 book on jurisdiction and administration in civil and canon law. What is strange about the book is the grandiose way in which the author resolved the problem of the independence – or better, perhaps, the dependence – of the judge, especially as he recognized beyond any doubt the problematical character of the procedure. For him the guarantees of the independence of the ecclesiastical judge are the 'inner authority of the papal and episcopal office and the tradition' and, in addition, the 'far-reaching control' of the Ordinary by the Holy See.[15] Melichar – and indeed also the well-known German canon lawyer Klaus Mörsdorf, who in 1941 published his important book on legal judgments and administration in Canon Law[16] – saw the parallel between the constitutional structure of the church and Fascist models of state, society and law. Melichar, for example, referred to the historical parallels between the unity of powers in Canon Law and in German Nazi law;[17] and in Mörsdorf's view, Fascist Italy had a 'hierarchical leadership' which welded individuals and social groups together into unity.[18] Melichar certainly wanted 'the fine distinction' to be borne in mind that 'in the one case . . . the fundamental fullness of power was maintained for dogmatic reasons' whereas 'in the other case . . . a dictator' resorted to 'increasingly drastic means'.[19] The authorities of the Catholic Church have never expressed any disapproval of these and similar comparisons between the constitution of the Catholic Church and Fascist models of order, or rejected them. However, they have done and still do so when church members speak of or even demand a democratizing of the church!

It is undeniable that from the twelfth century church authorities, and especially the papacy, have drawn comparisons between church structure and authoritarian models of the state and, indeed, even flirted with forms of government like monarchy, autocracy, or the 'strong state' (dictatorship). These ideas and this wishful thinking culminated in the development of the 'perfect society ideology' of the nineteenth century in which the state and the (Catholic) church are perfect societies. Even in the new 1983 Code this defective, because untheological, thinking about the church occupies a central, if hidden, place in c.204 §2. Until such time that the Catholic Church has definitively taken its leave of this ideology, efficient control of the exercise of power will ultimately be impossible and the realization of human rights within the church must continue to be restricted.

Against this background, the influence of basic or human rights within the Catholic Church will need to be assessed realistically. We have already noted that these basic rights suffer restrictions and suspensions through the voluntary bond of the individual to the inner ordering of the church. However, the church authorities will have to be very careful not to make the church's right to self-determination so wide that it involves a clear denial of basic rights. We cannot simply begin with the assumption 'that the church's right to self-determination suspends the force of basic rights'.[20] It is true that these basic rights will have to find their specific shape, application and recognition in the church sphere, within the setting of the church's self-understanding. However, they cannot now be created all over again for the (Catholic) church and by this church. Basic and human rights are quite evident norms to which people of an earlier age might have attached and in fact did attach the predicates 'of natural law' or 'absolute'.

In the 1983 Code there are also some disturbing inroads into basic rights. On the one hand we read in the catalogue of basic rights, more precisely in c.221 §3: 'The Christian faithful have the right not to be punished with canonical penalties except in accord with the norm of law.' This corresponds more or less to the age-old legal rule: '*Nulla poena sine lege poenali* (No penalty without a penal law)'. On the other hand, the new Code, in its Book on Sanctions in the Church, stipulates that a judge can punish more severely than 'a law or a precept has stated' (c.1326). This is an infringement of the rules of legal logic as well as of the systematics of law! Moreover, the stipulation is not found in the section on 'the imposition of penalties', where it belongs, but in the section dealing with 'punishable acts'.

This tension becomes somewhat understandable when we study the history of its development. The content of today's canon 221 §3 began with the long-projected Fundamental Law of the Church (*Lex Ecclesiae Fundamentalis* LEF). In the preparatory phase of the LEF, and after a great deal of discussion, it was inserted into the 1971 draft (c.21) by the appropriate Papal Commission. The text stated clearly: 'No one may be punished except in those cases circumscribed by the law itself and in the modes determined by it' (c.21).[21] In the 1976 Draft of the LEF, made public only in 1978, c.21 was reformulated to read: 'the faithful have the right not to be punished with canonical penalties, except in accord with the prescript of law'.[22]

When the project of an independent promulgation of the LEF was finally abandoned, the materials which had been treated in its draft form were taken up into the new Code. In the process, c.21 of the LEF underwent a new mutation. Canon 221 §3 now read: 'The Christian faithful have the right not to be punished with canonical penalties except in accord with the norm of law.' A comparison of the three texts illustrates how hesitantly the ecclesiastical legislator confronted this fundamental right.

2. Deficiencies of a general nature

After this critical appraisal of the regard for, and validity of, human or basic rights in the Catholic Church, I shall now advance more general considerations and wishes: church order and church law cannot and should not stand in opposition to the basic and human rights that prevail in civil society. Friendly and impartial relationships exist in most countries between state and church, and in some countries concordats exist as well. The church has to remember that out of this state of affairs an obligation arises for it to respect the legal value-system of the democratic state and to ensure that its own legal system is not too far removed from it.

A further problem which also touches upon the church's internal life may be signalled here. The Declaration on Human Rights of 1789, arising from a middle-class revolution, guaranteed the freedoms of the individual, but did not give more than peripheral attention to the safeguarding of social concerns. At the same time the French National Constituent Assembly unanimously decreed the death penalty for anyone who intended to propose a law which would deny the right of private property.[23] French theologians themselves later called attention to these flaws in the 1789 Declaration on the Rights of Man. Teilhard de Chardin, in his 'Reflections on the Rights of Man', originally published in 1947,[24] urged the setting-up of 'a system of organo-psychic solidarity on earth'. 'Collectivization and individualization,' he concluded, 'are thus not two opposed principles.'[25] The French canon lawyer L. de Naurois gave a similar judgment some years later.[26] Political institutions in the West, rather than the churches, also recognized the necessity for the establishment of social or collective human rights. One piece of evidence for this is the 1961 Social Charter of the Council of Europe, although much has still to be done to realize it. The churches could play a decisive role towards a universal heightening of conscience in this matter and, in addition, set a good example by conceiving a declaration of basic or human rights which takes account of social concerns.

Still more important, however, is another question which arises in our day in the face of our world-wide structures. Is there any call today for the establishing of human rights from the side of Christian theologians, given – as I conceded at the beginning of this article – that it is difficult to legitimize human rights from scripture, and that the history of Christianity bears witness to countless failures to observe human rights?

Wolfgang Huber and Heinz Eduard Tödt[27] believe that this question must be answered in the affirmative. The establishing of human rights must take place, they believe, as a necessary contribution of Christian theology towards an ethic of communication which must be discussed between Christians and non-Christians. When, therefore, Christian theologians, and in particular H. Küng, engage in dialogue with represent-atives of other religions on this very question, they are making pioneering contributions towards a totally new way of understanding religions. However, the promptings of Huber and Tödt still reveal a strong Christianity-centred assessment of the problem, though they were made some years ago now. In the dialogue with other religions Christian theologians will recognize more sharply the values but also the deficiencies which the Jewish-Christian tradition attests and preserves in relation to human rights. The theologians and other representatives of the various religions can make convincing contributions towards a necessary, or at the least a desirable, establishing of human rights only if these rights are also acknowledged and practised within institutionalized religion(s).

Translated by Leo C. Hay

Notes

1. L. Baudin, *Der sozialistische Staat der Inka*, Hamburg 1956. This book had already appeared in Paris in 1944, without source references and under the title *Les Incas du Pérou*.

2. H.-H. Schrey, 'Wiedergewinnung des Humanum? Menschenrechte in christ-licher Sicht', *Theologische Rundschau* 48, 1983, 68.

3. C. Westermann, in J. Baur (ed.), *Zum Thema Menschenrechte. Theologische Versuche und Entwürfe*, Stuttgart 1977.

4. Schrey, 'Wiedergewinnung' (n.2), 66 (with a reference to Heinrich Vogel).

5. W. Huber, *Evangelisches Staatslexikon*, Stuttgart ³1987, I, 2117. Cf also M. Pilters and K. Walf, *Menschenrechte in der Kirche*, Düsseldorf 1980 (with a comprehensive international bibliography). Schrey, 'Wiedergewinnung' (n.2), provides later and wider German-language literature, especially from the Protestant field. The following publications are also important: P. Hinder, *Grundrechte in der Kirche*, Freiburg CH (and bibliography); J. Neuman and M. W. Fischer (eds.), *Toleranz und Repression – Zur Lage religiöser Minderheiten in modernen Gesellschaften*, Frankfurt and New York 1987; and *Human Rights – International Bibliography 1975–1981*, *CERDIC*, Strasbourg 1982 (incomplete!).

6. The negative attitude of the nineteenth-century popes to human rights can be documented from many sources. See for example the encyclical *Mirari vos* of Gregory XVI of 15 August 1832 in which the pope, without naming names, rejected ideas of the French theologian Lamennais, e.g. absolute freedom of conscience and of the press and the rebellion of subjects against the sovereign. This latter situation is seen as equivalent to a rebellion against God, 'since freedom does not mean a severance from all bonds and the independence advocated by many leads to separation from church and state'. In his encyclical *Singulari nos* of 24 June 1834 Gregory confirmed his rejection of notions of freedom and democracy. His successor, Pius IX, in the encyclical *Quanta cura* of 8 December 1864 and his famous *Syllabus* of the same date, rejected a series of demands in the Declaration on Human Rights as irreconcilable with the Catholic faith.

7. M. Kaiser, in J. Listl, H. Müller and H. Schmitz (eds.), *Handbuch des katholischen Kirchenrechts*, Regensburg 1983, 174.

8. Behind the word *societas* used in the canon lies the ideology of the *societas perfecta* according to which the state and the Catholic Church are seen as 'perfect' societies.

9. *Pacem in terris*, no. 41.

10. How this stipulation is to be applied in practice is another question. One might think of the moderators of the so-called Central Committee of German Catholics who regularly occupy leading positions in the Christian parties.

11. K. Walf, 'Zur parteipolitischen Tätigkeit der Priester', *Frankfurter Hefte* 29, 1974, 397–400.

12. *Pastoral Constitution on the Church in the Modern World* 73, 2; 59, 4.

13. See e.g. the 1948 Universal Declaration of Human Rights (p. 9 above), article 18 (freedom of opinion appears in article 19.1).

14. W. Rüfner, 'Die Geltung von Grundrechten im kirchlichen Bereich', in *Essener Gespräche zum Thema Staat und Kirche* 7, Münster 1972, 9–27.

15. E. Melichar, *Gerichtsbarkeit und Verwaltung im staatlichen und kanonischen Recht*, Vienna 1948, 72.

16. K. Mörsdorf, *Rechtsprechung und Verwaltung im kanonischen Recht*, Freiburg 1941.

17. Melichar, *Gerichtsbarkeit* (n.15), 72. A resolution to this effect passed in the Nazi-dominated German Reichstag of 26 April 1942 is quoted at length in 73 n.152, giving the impression that Melichar approves this kind of legal thinking.

18. Mörsdorf, *Rechtsprechung* (n.16), 16f.

19. Melichar, *Gerichtsbarkeit* (n.15), 73.

20. Rüfner, 'Geltung' (n.14), 26.

21. *Herder-Korrespondenz* 25, 1971, 242.

22. *Herder-Korrespondenz* 32, 1978, 625.

23. Baudin, *Staat* (n.1), 12.

24. P. Teilhard de Chardin, 'Some Reflections on the Rights of Man', in *The Future of Man*, London and New York 1964, 193–5.

25. Ibid., 194.

26. L. de Naurois, 'Études des droits de l'homme', *Revue de droit canonique* XIV, 1964, (221–240) 224f.

27. W. Huber and H. E. Tödt, *Menschenrechte – Perspektiven einer menschlichen Welt*, Stuttgart and Berlin ²1978).

Human Rights and Islam: Foundation, Tradition, Violation

Roger Garaudy

No study of human rights in Islam, of the basis of the rights on the one hand and of the historical societies which appeal to its principles on the other, should ever lose sight of the following facts:

1. Islam is not a new religion, born with the preaching of the prophet Muhammad. The Qur'an includes him expressly in the line of Abraham, indivisibly Jewish, Christian and Muslim. According to the Qur'an, Islam (that is, obedience to Allah) began with the first man, with Adam into whom God 'breathed His spirit' (15, 21). The basis of human rights in Islam is the same as that of all revealed religions: the transcendent dimension of human beings.

2. Historically, in communities or states that appeal to the Qur'anic revelation, the constant temptation to sacralize power has led to an instrumentalization of religion, allowing divine law (*shari'a*) to be shaped to the needs of the prince, thus creating a tradition (*sunna*) which is sometimes in radical contradiction to the revelation. In this way was created what might by analogy be called a 'Muslim Constantinianism' appealing to the authority of religion to justify the worst violations of human rights.

I. The basis of 'human rights' according to the Qur'an

1. Islam is not a new religion. Allah commanded Muhammad: 'Say: I am no innovation among messengers' (46, 9); 'We have sent messengers before you' (14, 30). 'If you have any doubt over what we have revealed to you, seek among those of our messengers whom we sent before you' (43, 45). 'Allah has prescribed for you the religion which we have revealed to you and which we enjoined on Abraham, Moses and Jesus . . . be not divided therein' (42, 13). As for Jesus, in the Qur'an he occupies a place beyond the prophets: born of a Virgin, of the Virgin Mary, he is not Allah, but 'Jesus, the Messiah, is the messenger of Allah, and the fulfilment of glad tidings which he conveyed to Mary, and a mercy from him' (4, 171). 'We gave him the Gospel which contained guidance and light' (5, 46). The birth of Jesus is like the creation of Adam '. . . For Allah, Adam and Jesus are as one . . . Allah said: "Be, and he began to be"' (3, 59).

2. *'Human rights' based on the relation of human beings to the absolute have a theological orientation* similar to that of St Thomas: talk of 'natural law' (*fitra*), nature, in the Qur'an as in St Thomas carries within it its own finality: every being has an end willed by God. 'Our Lord has bestowed on each thing his form and his law (*gadar*), and he has guided it towards its full blossoming' (87, 13).

3. *Human beings alone have the awesome privilege of disobeying.* While all beings obey God's law through necessity, when human beings obey this law of God, they do so freely; 'We have proposed this mandate (*amana*) to the heavens, the earth and the mountains. All have refused to accept it, all have been afraid of accepting it. Man alone has accepted to undertake it' (33, 7). This is why Allah makes the angels bow before him (2, 34). The price paid for this freedom is human injustice in refusing God's guidance. Human beings have the possibility of it and the responsibility for it: 'We have shown him the right way, he is either appreciative and follows it or is ungrateful and rejects it' (76, 3). For human beings, faith is an act of free will: 'This is the truth from your Lord; then let him who will, believe, and let him who will, disbelieve' (18, 29).

Prophets have been sent to every nation (35, 4) speaking the language of each nation (35, 24)[1] to remind them of God's will. Freedom of conscience must be respected. 'There shall be no compulsion in religion' (2, 256). 'There shall be no compulsion in religion' is the basic axiom which enables us to understand why, when the word *jihad* (which means 'effort', and which is incorrectly translated as 'holy war') is used twenty-one times in the Qur'an, violence is not excluded, but never for the purpose of *spreading* religion. It is tolerated only to defend it against those who wish to oppose it.

4. *The universalist spirit follows from divine unity* (*tawhid*): humanity is one because God, its creator, is One.

The Prophet created at Medina a radically new type of community (*umma*): it was not founded on blood and race, nor on the possession of territory, nor on commercial links, nor even on a common language, history or culture. In a word, it is not based on anything which follows from nature or from the past, on anything which is a given heritage. It is a community based exclusively on faith, on the unconditional response to the call of God, of which Abraham is the eternal example.

Nothing, for example, conflicts more with the spirit of this *umma* than the Western idea of nationalism, and even of the 'nation', that is, the idea of a market protected by a state and justified by a racial, historic, cultural mythology, striving to make the nation an end in itself.

It is significant that in the Muslim world 'nationalism' has always been theorized by non-Muslims: the Arab nationalism of the 'Baas' of Iraq and Syria by the Christian Michel Aflak, as previously Turkish nationalism by the Jew Vambéry. These forms of nationalism are imports of European colonialism: the 'Arab League' is an old English dream fulfilled in order to dismantle the Ottoman Empire, and which outlived colonialism to sustain the divisions of the *umma*.

5. *The principles of the rights of the community of Medina, at the time of the Prophet, strictly derive from 'divine law'* (shari'a).

(*a*) Economic law is based on the principle: Allah alone possesses. Man, his representative (*calif*) on earth, is given the responsibility of managing this property, in Allah's way.

This concept is the opposite of Roman law, which defines property as 'the right to use and to abuse'. For the Muslim, on the other hand, duties come before rights. Property is therefore a discretionary, not an absolute right.

Human beings, the managers responsible for Allah's property, cannot dispose of it at will: they cannot destroy it according to a whim; they cannot squander it, let it lie fallow without making it bear fruit by their labour; they cannot accumulate it: 'Warn those who hoard up gold and silver and spend it not in the cause of Allah of a painful chastisement' (9, 34). And the worst curse in the Qur'an is that pronounced on the rich Abu Lahab, condemned by his very fortune: 'May both his hands perish, and may he himself perish and be consigned to the infernal flames' (Surah 3).

All the dictates of the Qur'an, notably the *zakat*, the social transfer of wealth as a religious requirement, and the banning of the *riba*, namely of any increase in wealth unaccompanied by work in the service of Allah, tend to prevent the accumulation of wealth at one pole of society and poverty at the other.

In the Qur'an, Allah radically excludes any social system in which money creates a political hierarchy. On the contrary, he says unequivocally: 'Before we decide to destroy a township . . . we make the rich the holders of power' (27, 16).

(b) The right to knowledge is based on the principle that Allah alone knows. This excludes any claim to be in possession of complete, definitive, and absolute knowledge, a claim which necessarily leads to the examination of those who do not recognize the authority of such servants of the absolute. 'Everything I say about God is said by a man,' wrote Karl Barth. This critical humility is the best antidote to dogmatism.

(c) Political law is based on the principle that Allah alone commands. It is not a matter of 'theocracy' as in the mediaeval West, that is to say, of the domination of the church. As a matter of principle, the Qur'an excludes all mediation between the believer and Allah and consequently any clergy or monarchy 'by divine right'.

Such a concept challenges those 'defenders of human rights' who, though appealing to Rousseau, have forgotten his fundamental warnings on the smooth running of a democracy whose two major pitfalls he denounced: the inequality of wealth which destroys 'the general will' for the benefit of the wealthy, and the absence of a faith in absolute values, without which the desires of individuals and groups (as externally of nations) for power, expansion and enjoyment are in endless conflict.

Rousseau appeared to discern in advance the evils inherent in any 'liberal democracy', namely that, as in former days in Athens, it led to the domination of a wealthy oligarchy under cover of a statistical, delegated, alienated democracy.

Strangely, the term 'democracy' is given to the slave-run oligarchy of Pericles, where 20,000 'free' citizens ruled over 110,000 slaves deprived of any rights, but after Rousseau, the same imposture affected 'human rights'.

The American Declaration of Independence and the French Revolution's Declaration of the Rights of Man and of the Citizen proclaimed: 'All men are born free with equal rights'. The former was to retain the slavery of blacks for a century. The latter was to deprive more than half the French nation of the right to vote as 'passive citizens' because they had no property. According to Diderot's axiom, 'No one is a citizen without property'.

Rousseau did not share the hypocritical illusion of the early nineteenth-century 'liberal' economists, according to which if everyone pursues his individual interest the general interest will spontaneously be guaranteed. Nearly two centuries' experience of this system have denounced this falsehood: a primitive confrontation of egoisms leads to an outcome desired by no one and assures the supremacy of those who wield the economic powers of constraint, manipulation of opinion or corruption.

The only postulate on which a society truly capable of producing a 'general will' can reside is that of the 'virtue' of each citizen. In order to guarantee this, Rousseau demanded a 'profession of faith', declaring that men living in society need a religion which will uphold them in it. 'No nation has ever survived nor will survive without religion. . . . In any state which can require its members to sacrifice their life, the one who does not believe in the life to come is necessarily a coward or a madman' (p. 336).

'It is important to the state that every citizen should have a religion which makes him respect his civil duties.'

The 'profession of faith' that Rousseau demands of every citizen, which does not refer to any particular religion but to the first and fundamental religion, strongly resembles Islam, not as presented by its traditions, but as revealed in the Qur'an.

'The dogmas of civil religion,' wrote Rousseau, 'must be simple, few in number: the existence of a powerful, intelligent, beneficent, provident Divinity; the life to come; the happiness of the just and the punishment of the wicked; the sanctity of the social contract and of laws. And the rejection of intolerance' (p. 341).

Of the political system which he advocated in *The Social Contract* Rousseau says: 'It is a kind of *theocracy* in which the state should have no other priests than its magistrates.'

It is indeed a 'theocracy' but, unlike the 'theocracies' known in the West, God does not reign through the mediation of a clergy or a monarchy regarded as sacred. God reigns in the heart of each member of the community. This, instead of creating an absolute power (totalitarian in the full sense of the word, that is to say governing souls as well as bodies, the interior as well as the exterior), on the contrary makes all power, all possessions, all knowledge relative.

'Allahu Akbar!' (Allah is greater) carries within it a subversive charge. In the face of this inflexible certainty of a people so sure of their faith, one could see the arms of the most arrogant armies being lowered. There is no power 'with divine right'. A *hadith* quotes these words of the Prophet: 'There is no holier war than to tell the truth to an unjust tyrant.' This 'theocracy' is therefore truly a 'democracy' in which Allah speaks through each member of the community. The Qur'an demands that no power should be exercised without 'dialogue' (*shura*).

How could this liberating revelation have through the centuries reverted to an enslaving tradition?

II. Tradition and violation of duties and rights

The *shari'a* (divine law) governs by its principles all human relationships, from economics to politics and from the inner life to conjugal relations, from the perspective of faith in an omnipresent and omniscient God whom no one can deceive. The *shari'a* (that is etymologically: 'the path to the source') then consists of living one's public and private life, twenty-four hours a day, in the sight of Allah.

But historically, in the practice of states, that is not the case.

The will to perpetuate the established powers has, through the centuries and up to the present day, led to three cardinal perversions of Islam which have led in turn to the violation of human rights: literalism, the growth of the *hadith* (words or behaviour attributed to the Prophet), and an idolatrous cult of tradition, at times placed above the Qur'anic revelation although contradicting it.

1. Literalism consists of reading the Qur'an with the eyes of the dead, as though being a Muslim meant living like a tenth-century Arab subject to the Abbassides and according to their laws.

The desire to read the Qur'an 'according to the letter' is to forget that the God of Abraham revealed himself in a story. This in no way contradicts the absolute. God intervenes, in the Qur'an as in the Bible, in order to bring concrete responses to historic situations out of absolute, eternal principles.

One cannot therefore 'deduce' from verses in the Qur'an isolated from their historical context a constitution or a legal code, as did Bossuet in his *Politics drawn from the Scriptures* or, in Islam, El Mawerdi in his treatise *On Power*. Both cases lead to the justification of an absolute monarchy, that of Louis XIV or that of the Abbassides.

Such is the root and definition of any 'integralism': the identification of faith with the cultural or institutional form which it assumed at such an outmoded period of its history.

On the contrary, it is a question of freeing from their immediate realization the eternal principles which will enable one to arrive at a solution of present-day problems.

The Qur'an always reveals to us the goals to pursue: it is the responsibility of the people of each century to find the means of reaching them.

From the fundamental aims of the Qur'an assigned to man by divine revelation, a dialogue (*shura*) can be set up which will respond, in a spirit of creative responsibility and initiative, to the challenges of our time.

The Qur'an contains 6,236 verses: only 228 are devoted to legal prescriptions, of which 70 concern the family, 70 the civil code, 13 jurisdiction and procedure, 10 constitutional law, 10 the economic and financial order, 25 international relations, 30 the penal code.

In total, 3% of the Qur'an concerns the law, and 0.05% penal law, while nearly the whole of the Qur'an deals with faith and morality, 'the true way', that is to say the goals to be followed to achieve the way of Allah.

Without any doubt a radical break with the legislation inherited from colonialism (mostly English and French) is absolutely necessary, for it had been developed from a conception of the world and human beings which was unacceptable to an Islamic society, fundamentally because it disregards the transcendent human dimension and contents itself with checking or channelling the rival appetites of an individualistic society where brother will turn on brother.

But the essential change cannot be brought about by substituting for these codes the literal and fragmentary application of another code aimed at a realization of absolute principles in the historical conditions of the Arab world as it existed a thousand years ago.

A true 'application of the *shari'a*' has nothing to do with this lazy literalism.

It implies that behind each prescription of the Qur'an or Sunna can be found its *raison d'être*, the principle which was its inspiration and the historic conditions in which it was applied.

Above all, even more importantly, each of these processes must be placed within the totality of the Qur'anic revelation.

It is, for example, obtuse literalism to consider that 'cutting off the hand of a thief' (5, 38) is characteristic of the *shari'a*, although it constitutes a violation of human rights and dignity.

The real problem faced by the Prophet at Medina, in an exemplary way and in historic conditions, was to devise the 'penal code' in the context of social justice so that theft would have no further place and consequently the punishment would have no relevance.

This is so true that one of the Prophet's closest companions, 'Umar, when he became Calif, considered that the punishment of cutting off a hand did not apply in time of famine, when it was not possible to impose social justice.

Two of the most authoritative collections of *hadith*, those of An Nasai and Abu Dawud, recall the Prophet Muhammad's stance on this point: A slave has stolen wheat from a field. The owner demands the punishment. The Prophet summons the master of the slave: 'This man was hungry and you did not feed him. You are the one whom I shall punish.' And the *hadith* adds: 'The messenger of Allah gave the slave a measure of wheat.' It is clear that in original Islam, that of the Qur'an and of the Prophet Muhammad, social justice is a moral value superior to the defence of property.

Nothing is more contradictory to the spirit of the Qur'an than to apply a system of punishments before improving social justice.

The Qur'an and the Sunna organize the redistribution of wealth: the Qur'an institutes the *zakat*, that is to say, not voluntary charity, but an obligatory levy, not on income but on wealth: in general the Sunna fixes the rate at 2.5% for non-invested money (only the means of production are excluded). A simple calculation shows that at this rate a fortune is completely wiped out in forty years, in a generation, so that no one can live off the wealth inherited from parents. In a country where these prescriptions were rigorously applied, Allah's law, the true *shari'a*, would begin to reign on the economic and social plane, and the thief could only be a sick person, as there would no longer be any 'need' which could lead to theft. If on the other hand one starts with repression, the poorest will suffer the most, while the 'hoarders of money' denounced by the Qur'an, like today's Arabian princes, will continue to accumulate in the United States billions of dollars which are not used in 'the service of Allah'. In order not to be trapped in a literal reading it is essential, over and beyond the layers of 1200 years of commentaries, scholasticism, formalism and tailoring the message to what suited the first dynasties centuries ago, that we rediscover the Qur'an itself in its entirety and its spirit, even if this runs counter to 'tradition'. For we cannot put the Qur'an, which is divine word, and tradition, which is human word, on the same plane. We have no right to let the divine word be obscured by the human word.

The Qur'an itself teaches us this distancing and this humility, when it says that beyond what Allah has revealed to him, the prophet is a man like any other: 'Say: I am only a man like you' (18, 3; 41, 6). 'You are but an admonisher; you have no authority to compel them' (88, 21–22).

The drama of Islam stems from this: for over a thousand years there has been a tendency to blur the dividing line between the human and the divine word, between the revelation of the universal message and the tradition peculiar to a particular race at a certain moment in its history.

2. The increase in *hadith* and their commentaries, debated for centuries, is the second reason for the corruption of the message. Let us just take one example: that of 'predestination'. The *hadith*, in giving a fatalistic and resigned interpretation of certain verses of the Qur'an, showing on the contrary that all freedom derives from Allah, began to proliferate during

the period of the Umayyads (660–750), that is, at a period when pious Muslims became indignant at the wild behaviour of their lords, far removed from the Qur'anic ideal. In order, therefore, to maintain obedience among the people, it was necessary to draw from 'tradition' a doctrine affirming that Allah had decreed from all eternity that these people should rule; that their turpitude and crimes were part of a destiny ordained by Allah.

The courtly poets exalted their princes as sovereigns 'whose domination had already been decreed in the eternal decrees of Allah'. 'Predestination' was the theological guarantee of injustice and tyranny: the opium of the people. It will often be thus in Islam, in radical contradiction to the Qur'an, where it is written: 'Lord, we obeyed our leaders and great ones and they led us astray from the right path. Lord, intensify their punishment and deprive them utterly of your mercy' (33, 67–68).

In a more familiar and popular manner, one *hadith* relates that the Prophet, having seen a bedouin at prayer leaving his camel unfettered, pointed out that he thus risked losing the animal. The man replied that that depended on the will of Allah. 'Tie up your camel,' said the Prophet, 'and trust in Allah.'

This remark reveals the profound meaning of the expression: 'Insh Allah' (if Allah wills). It takes away nothing from our own responsibility: it prohibits all 'self-importance': the sailor does not make the wind blow, but it is up to him to unfurl the sails.

3. This accumulation of false *hadith*, born in a period of despotism and carefully conserved by all the powers and by servile commentators, became petrified for more than a thousand years, forming a wall preventing the masses from going back to the Qur'an as a source.

Two examples will serve to illustrate this perverse contradiction between the Qur'anic revelation and tradition.

(*a*) Punishment of blasphemy

First, the call by Ayatollah Khomeini for the execution of the author of a blasphemous book.

In the Abrahamic religions (Jewish, Christian, Muslim) blasphemy is the greatest of crimes, a crime against the spirit. The Jewish *torah* demands the stoning to death of the blasphemer (Leviticus 24.13–16). It is in the name of this verse that the high priest calls for Jesus' death: 'You have heard the blasphemy . . . And they all condemned him to be guilty of death' (Mark 14.64).

In the Gospel according to St Matthew it is said of the blasphemer: 'It shall not be forgiven him, neither in this world, neither in the world to come' (12, 32).

On this point, the Qur'an takes up the Gospel word for word: 'Allah curses them in this life and in the next' (33.8). It is evident, then, as the Qur'an makes clear (6, 62), that 'it is for Allah alone to judge'. So Ayatollah Khomeini did not base his call on the Qur'an but on a tradition which contradicts the Qur'an, and which takes up the ancient law which restoring to human beings the responsibility of judging and punishing.

(b) The condition of women

The condition of women in Muslim countries under a despotic regime is another example of this violation of rights.

One must first set aside a crushing weight of prejudices, slogans, incitement to fear and to hatred of Islam.

The West also has hypocritical reasons to be indignant, for in subtler forms the violation of women's rights is evident there. Women's participation in economic activity has, since the beginnings of capitalism in Europe, become a participation 'in the labour market', as cheap labour. The disparity in remuneration for equal qualifications still remains flagrant in industry today. The proportion of women occupying managerial positions remains far lower than that of men (2% of women among managers of large or medium enterprises).

Even when it does not constitute pornography, the commercial utilization of sexuality in advertising, the press, the cinema and publishing makes women, reduced to their bodies, a commodity and a consumer product.

Thus a degraded vision of love is communicated to youth, separating sexuality from the meaning of life.

And even legitimate protests against polygamy would be more credible if they did not come from a Western world where the law stipulates monogamy and polygamy is practised.

It is nonetheless true that in Islam today there is flagrant violation of the rights of women. This derives not from the message of the Qur'an, but from the traditional way of life in the Near East.

The Qur'an, like the Bible, should be read in the historical context which illuminates its formulations linked to the level of understanding of the people, and which enables one to distinguish the absolute principle from which a historical response was made at such a stage in its development.

From that moment on one can see the true significance of the verses of the Qur'an which speak of the 'pre-eminence of man' (2, 228). This idea of 'pre-eminence' is linked to an established family structure. This means the affirmation of an ontological superiority of men over women, with the attempt to justify it by a puerile psychology attributing eternal weaknesses to women. This leads to absurdities which Ibn Hazm of Cordova brought out. Simply because he is of male sex, is a man *a priori* superior to the mother of Abraham, of Moses, of Jesus, whom the Qur'an tells us received direct messages from God, as did the Prophets, warning them of the birth and destiny of their sons (11, 71–73; 28, 7; 19, 19), or superior to Khadiyya who received the first revelation of the Prophet, or to Aïsha to whom the Sunna tells us Moslems owe half of their religious teaching?

Among human beings there is no other superiority than that of piety, of obedience to Allah. Ibn Hazm emphasizes (*Fisal*, Vol. IV, p. 126) that when the Qur'an speaks of 'men', by that it means all human beings, and not only the masculine sex.

Any discrimination belongs to the history of a country or to a period in that country's history, indicating a breach with the Qur'an. On eight occasions (3, 95; 4, 124; 13, 23; 17, 40; 40, 40; 43, 17; 48, 6; 57, 18) the Qur'an reminds us that Allah makes no distinction between human beings, be they men or women, except between those who do good and those who do wrong.

Beyond all the vicissitudes of history the eternal principle is thus affirmed, abolishing all hierarchy between man and woman, instituting not only their 'equality' or their 'complementarity', but their 'ontological' unity: 'Your Lord created you from one single being', says the first verse of the Surah 'Women' (4, 1). There is a single being divided in two, equal in dignity and differing only in their functions. Outside this fundamental principle of the message, which does not justify any discrimination, everything is a matter of tradition and historical conjecture.

The problem of polygamy is significant. First, it was not instituted by the Qur'an, which on the contrary limited it. For example, the message excludes the 'harem' which the Bible attributes to David, or the 700 wives of Solomon, not to mention his 300 concubines (I Kings 11.1–3), or even the unlimited polygamy which existed in pre-Islamic Arabia.

The Qur'an does not prohibit polygamy, although it imposes conditions which make it very impracticable: 'If you feel that you will not deal justly between them, then marry only one' (4, 3). 'Allah has not made for any man two hearts in his bosom' (33, 4).

Once again, before judging in a peremptory and abstract way, one should become informed about the historical context of Greek, Roman and even Christian societies, where discrimination concerning women demands that women be subject to their husbands (I Peter 3.1) and that they be silent in churches (I Corinthians 14.34), so that they should not be suspected of being closer to matter and sin.

The Qur'an contains recommendations which are shocking only if judged beyond the bounds of the social structures of an established society, as for example the law of succession.

Bearing in mind the fact that, in Arab society, all obligations concerning the maintenance of family and relations, and everything which we would today call 'social security' are the responsibility of the husband, the share of the inheritance for the son is double that of the daughter (4, 2).

In societies where the woman has the same social responsibilities as the man, justice obviously cannot be carried out in the same way. There too, the literal observance of a verse taken out of its historical context would lead to a violation of the fundamental spirit of the revelation.

There is nothing in the Qur'an which can justify the discrimination against the veritable 'apartheid' of woman which reigns today in many Muslim countries: this discrimination issues from a certain Near Eastern tradition and in no way from Islam. In Islam at the time of the Prophet and the 'well guided' caliphs, although a division of labour and duties was observed, women were not excluded from any social activity. They managed businesses (Bukhari, 11, 40). The caliph 'Umar appointed a woman superintendent of the market at Medina. Aisha, the Prophet's wife, taught theology. The caliph 'Umar did not take offence at having his sermon interrupted by a woman, and even thanked her for the exactness of her criticism: ' 'Umar is wrong,' he said, 'and the woman is right.'

Wearing the veil is a pre-Islamic tradition of the Near East: Byzantine icons show that seven centuries before the Hegira the Virgin Mary wore the veil which is still worn today by the women of that region. The Qur'an ratifies this tradition, but its fundamental message, beyond local traditions, is that women should not use their physical attributes, be it their faces, their figures, their breasts or their legs, to seduce men, distracting them from carrying out their duties. This decency does not imply a 'fashion' peculiar to a given country, but a moral code of behaviour, not linked to any particular mode of dress.

Even the word which in the Qur'an designates 'veil' (*hijab*) stems from the verb meaning 'to conceal', whether it be to conceal one's thoughts or one's charms. It does not therefore correspond to any particular form of clothing.

All forms (or even symbols, like the veil) of segregation and subordination of woman come from a tradition, if not from a folklore, of the Near East, and not from the message of the Qur'an.

These are only a few examples of a more general truth: violations of human rights in historical and contemporary Islam result not from the universalist message of the Qur'an but from its corruption by particular traditions, notably from the Near East.

III. Conclusions

Respect for human rights in contemporary Islam demands that one goes back to draw from the living source of the revelation beyond dead traditions. This involves:

1. *Putting an end to the triumphalism* of a tradition, considering, in radical contradiction to the Qur'an, that Islam began with the preaching of the Prophet Muhammad and became fixed from that time on. This implies a triple closing-out: with regard to the past from earlier wisdom and revelations which are also messages from Allah; with regard to the future, from any effort to find, starting from eternal principles, ever-new solutions to ever-new problems that 'Allah does not stop creating', 'being present in all new things' (55, 29); with regard to the present from dialogue in the sorry certainty that our religion is the best because we are ignorant of any other.

2. *Putting an end to literalism and to the opposition to change* which that implies, if we recall how the Qur'an itself demands to be read: Allah speaks to man in history, that is, in calling for examples on which we must reflect (39, 27). It is not a matter of axioms from which one can deduce responses to everything and in all ages, but of examples which demand reasoning by analogy in order that the same principles may be applied in different, new situations.

Allah speaks to man through parables, upon which we must also reflect (14, 25; 30, 27; etc.). This symbolism necessarily issues from the transcendence of Allah which I can neither perceive through my senses nor imagine through my reason. Only in this way can there be reborn, from an Islam which has become scholastic and Talmudic among 'doctors of law', a living Islam with its own critical spirit and humility before Allah.

3. *Putting an end to legalism* which deprives Islam of its dimension of interiority and love.

For example, the Qur'an recognizes on a legal plane the concept of the *ius talionis* ('an eye for an eye . . .') which ruled in pre-Islamic Arabia, but it recalls the universal message: beyond law, which is rooted in history, there is a moral requirement, Allah's demand. If man today has a right to the *ius talionis*, he also has the duty, if he wishes to please a 'clement and merciful Allah', to obey the eternal unwritten law, that of Jesus, to 'repel evil with good' (Qur'an 28, 54).

Contrary to 'tradition', it is not true that the Qur'an excludes as anthropomorphic Allah's love of man and man's love of Allah: 'Verily my Lord is ever merciful, most loving (*wadud*)' (11, 90); 'Allah will bring a people whom He will love and who will love Him' (5, 54).

The great Sufis, from Rumi to Ibn Arabi, saw a theophany even in human love: 'It is in the book of human love,' wrote Ruzbehan of Shiraz, 'that one learns to comprehend divine love.' Ibn Arabi who, like Dante, had his Beatrice to guide him in his mystic ascent, strongly emphasized this continuity in his book of love: human love reveals to us that my centre is not in myself but in another, and the greatest love is the sacrifice of oneself for another.

It is no longer a question of an external, formal morality, of a submission to God akin to that of the slave to his master, where action and respect for another's rights are only inspired by fear of punishments of hell or the desire for the rewards of paradise, the slave-concept of Islam. For the Sufis, to fear Allah is to fear displeasing him, and that is called love, for Ghazzali as for Ibn Arabi.

This 'christic' dimension of love, counter to the withering teachings of the 'doctors of law', must be revived as an integral part of Islam.

To the revelation of God saying to Moses in the burning bush 'I am', Jesus adds this new dimension of the revelation: 'He is Love'.

A Muslim must not forget that the Qur'an takes up both of these revelations.

If Islam rejects the formulation of the Trinity defined at Nicaea in the language and culture of the Greeks, it must not omit the fact that Allah is not the abstract unity of Being, but the living unity of the relationship of love. The Persian mystic Ruzbehan of Shiraz and Ibn Arabi after him gave expression to this new concept: 'Before the existence and destiny of the world, Allah was the unity of love, of the loving and the loved.'

Such, for Muslims as for Christians, is the ultimate basis of human rights, not a nature nor a reason which would be prescribed to a particular end, but the necessity to struggle against everything which, for millions of human beings, through injustice, disfigures the face of God.

Islam, like Christianity, needs this theology of liberation.

Translated by Barrie Mackay

Note

1. Just as St Augustine wrote: 'One must not question that the Gentiles also have their prophets' (*Contra Faustum* XIX, 2).

Qur'an, Shari'a and Human Rights: Foundations, Deficiencies and Prospects

Abdullahi Ahmed An-Na'im

Notions affirming human dignity and some aspects of human rights in the modern sense of the term may be found in many historical, cultural and religious traditions. However, the full concept of human rights as rights to be accorded to every human being by virtue of being human is of very recent theoretical origin, and remains largely unrealized in practice. The crucial characteristic feature of the principle of human rights is that there should be rights to be accorded to every human being by virtue of being human and without discrimination on grounds of race, colour, sex, language, religion, etc. This principle was established by the Charter of the United Nations in 1945, and elaborated upon by the Universal Declaration of Human Rights of 1948 and subsequent instruments.

It is with reference to this fundamental principle that the Islamic tradition is examined in this article. Like other prophetic religions, Islam can be examined in terms of its basic scripture (the Qur'an), its theological and jurisprudential expression (Shari'a) and the actual practice of Muslims at any given period in history. All three aspects will be covered in the following brief discussion of the foundations, deficiencies and future prospects of human rights in the Muslim world.

I. The Qur'an

According to Muslim belief, the Qur'an is the literal and final word of God as revealed to the Prophet Muhammad between 610 and 632 CE. For the first thirteen years of his mission, the Prophet received and preached the precepts of Islam in and around Mecca. As a result of mounting persecution, the small community of Muslims migrated from Mecca to Medina, another town in western Arabia, in 622, where the Prophet established and ruled the first Islamic state until his death in 632. Throughout the duration of his mission, the Prophet explained and implemented the principles of the Qur'an through his own personal example and verbal utterances, commonly known as Sunna. During the first three centuries of Islam (seventh to the ninth centuries CE), Muslim scholars developed the principles of Shari'a out of the Qur'an (and Sunna as well as other traditions of the early Muslims). It is this Shari'a, rather than the pure texts of the Qur'an (and other sources), which has constituted the basis of Islamic civilizations since the seventh century.

When we consider the text of the Qur'an in terms of human rights as rights to be accorded to every human being by virtue of being human, we find that whereas some parts of the Qur'an provide sound foundations for human rights without discrimination, other parts tend to exclude women and non-Muslims. General principles of justice, equality and freedom, etc., without discrimination on grounds of race, colour, gender or religion, can be found in the Qur'an, especially at the earlier stage of revelation in Mecca. However, specific rules established by the Qur'an itself during the subsequent Medina stage of 622 to 632 CE clearly discriminate against women and non-Muslims. For example, whereas verses of the Qur'an of the Mecca stage emphasized freedom of belief and the equal dignity of all human beings regardless of faith or gender,[1] verses of the Medina stage imposed restrictions on the rights of women and non-Muslims.[2]

The early Muslim scholars resolved this apparent contradiction through the concept of *naskh* (abrogation) by deeming the subsequently revealed verses to have repealed or abrogated the earlier verses, for the purposes of Shari'a. As will be explained below, it may be possible now to reverse that process of abrogation in order to develop a modern version of Shari'a which guarantees equality for women and non-Muslims. Before doing so, however, we must candidly admit and identify the discrimination which exists under historical formulations of Shari'a. It would be misleading to cite those verses of the Qur'an which support equality and freedom of religion without mentioning those which do discriminate on grounds of gender and religion. Moreover, any discussion of human rights in Islam should not be confined to the bare text of the Qur'an. Reference must be made not only to the way in which the Qur'an has been interpreted, but also to Sunna and other sources of Shari'a, because this is the context in which the Qur'an is understood and applied by Muslims.

II. Historical Shari'a and human rights

The Arabic word 'Shari'a' is a noun derived from the verb *shari'a*, which means to set the path or road that provides access to a source. The term Shari'a may also mean way of life or method. The root and its derivatives are used in their general sense only in five verses of the Qur'an, namely 5:48, 7:163, 42:13, 42:21 and 45:18. In due course, however, the term Shari'a came to mean the 'divinely ordained Islamic way of life'. As such, it includes not only legal and jurisprudential matters, but also devotional rituals, theology, ethics, and even personal hygiene and good manners.[3]

We need not discuss the origins and development of Shari'a in detail here. What needs to be emphasized is that what is commonly known as Shari'a was the product of human understanding of the sources of Islam in the historical context of the seventh to the ninth centuries. During that period, Muslim jurists interpreted the Qur'an and other sources in order to develop a comprehensive and coherent system of Shari'a for the guidance of Muslim communities. If that historical formulation of Shari'a is to be applied today, it would violate many of the fundamental human rights of women and non-Muslims.[4]

The main human rights problems for women under Shari'a can be discussed under the rubric of equality before the law. While Shari'a recognized independent legal personality for women, it did not treat them as equals to men. The general rationale of women's inferiority to men under Shari'a is the principle of *qawama* whereby men are deemed to be the guardians of women. Based on verse 4:34 of the Qur'an, this principle has been taken as the basis for a variety of limitations on women's rights. For example, according to this principle of Shari'a, no woman may hold any public office which involves exercising authority over men. This would effectively deny all women access to high-ranking public office, regardless of their personal competence and qualifications. Moreover, because of this general principle and the specific rule contained in verse 2:282 of the Qur'an regarding testimonial competence, women are completely disqualified from being competent witnesses in serious criminal cases. In civil cases where women's testimony is accepted, it takes two women to make a single witness.

A number of other specific examples of women's inequality to men under Shari'a can be found in the areas of inheritance and family. As a general rule, a woman's share in inheritance is half the share of a man in accordance with verses 4:11 and 4:176 of the Qur'an. In family law, whereas a man is entitled to take up to four wives at the same time by virtue of verse 4:3 of the Qur'an, and to divorce any of them at will and without having to justify or explain his decision to any person or authority, a woman is restricted to one husband at a time and may only obtain judicial divorce on very specific grounds.[5]

In general, Shari'a was concerned with guaranteeing certain minimum rights for women rather than achieving equality between men and women. In terms of that limited objective, one finds that the position of women under Shari'a's was superior to their position under other legal systems prevailing up to the end of the nineteenth and early twentieth centuries.[6] However, from the point of view of complete equality between men and women required by modern human rights standards, Shari'a provisions are no longer adequate.

· Similarly, although the level of minimum rights achieved by Shari'a for non-Muslims is admirable in historical perspective, it is no longer adequate by modern human rights standards. Non-Muslims were classified by Shari'a into two main groups: believers, mainly Christians and Jews, and unbelievers. Believers, also known as People of the Book, were to be granted the status of *dhimma*, a compact with the Muslims which guarantees *dhimmis* security of person and property and the right to practice their faith in exchange for payment of poll tax (*jizya*) to the Muslim state. *Dhimmis* might conduct their own communal affairs in accordance with their own law, but they were subject to the jurisdiction of the Muslim state in public matters while being disqualified by Shari'a from holding any public office which involves exercising authority over Muslims. Unbelievers were generally not recognized as persons by Shari'a, but some of them may be granted *aman*, safe conduct, to reside in Muslim lands and, according to some jurists, long-term residents might be treated as *dhimmis*.[7]

Another aspect of Shari'a which violates freedom of religion and conscience as a human right is the notion of apostasy. According to Shari'a, whereas non-Muslims are to be encouraged to convert to Islam, it is a crime punishable by death for a Muslim to repudiate his faith in Islam. Beside its obvious discrimination against non-Muslims, this principle of Shari'a also violates the freedom of belief and expression of Muslims. As clearly illustrated by a recent case from the Sudan, a Muslim who expresses unorthodox views may be executed for apostasy.[8]

III. Contemporary Muslim Practice

Shari'a has been displaced by secular (mostly Western) law in most parts of the Muslim world for several generations now. Even countries such as Saudi

Arabia, which purport to implement Shari'a as the sole law of the land, now have significant non-Shari'a elements in their legal systems. Moreover, most Muslim countries have introduced guarantees of equality between men and women, freedom of religion, etc. in their domestic laws and constitutions. These countries have also endorsed the Universal Declaration of Human Rights and ratified some of the international human rights treaties. In view of all these developments, the above-noted objectionable principles of Shari'a are not directly applied in the vast majority of Muslim countries today.

Nevertheless, it would be an extremely serious mistake to underestimate the impact of these principles of Shari'a on human rights practice in the Muslim world. For one thing, Shari'a rules continue to apply in matters of family law and inheritance throughout the Muslim world. Consequently, all the provisions of Shari'a which violate the human rights of women in these fields are applied today in all Muslim countries. Furthermore, the so-called Islamic resurgence movements are demanding the immediate reinstatement of Shari'a as the sole law of the land in many Muslim countries. These movements have already succeeded in Iran, and are likely to succeed in other parts of the Muslim world. If and when these movements achieve political power, serious human violations are bound to follow.

The most serious negative impact of Shari'a on human rights in the Muslim world, however, is due to the strong influence Shari'a has on the attitudes and private conduct of most Muslims. So long as the above noted and other problematic aspects of Shari'a continue to be perceived as part of the 'divinely ordained Islamic way of life', they will continue to frustrate the formal commitment to human rights expressed by officials of the state. Constitutional and legal provisions and international commitments to human rights standards are not likely to have much impact in practice without sufficient Islamic legitimacy and popular support for these policies.

To illustrate this point, brief reference may be made to the recent case of Salman Rushdie. This man, a British citizen of Indian Muslim origins, wrote a novel entitled *The Satanic Verses*. Thousands of Muslims demonstrated and demanded that the book should be banned not only in their own countries, but also throughout the world. Moreover, many of the demonstrating Muslims called for the death of the author. Imam Khomeini of Iran called upon all Muslims to seek out and kill the author and any person associated with publication and sale of the book. Even after Rushdie apologized for the distress his book caused to Muslims, Imam

Khomeini insisted that even if he completely repented and recanted his views, Rushdie should nevertheless be killed. At least one moderate Muslim leader was killed because he spoke against the killing of Rushdie. Other violent actions against the author and other moderate Muslims may follow.

It is true that Imam Khomeini's action is contrary to Shari'a in that he condemned a man to death without trial and rejected defences to the charge of apostasy, the presumed offence in this case. However, it should also be noted that other Muslims did not condemn Khomeini's action. The reasons for this failure may include some political factors and a sense of Muslim solidarity against the West. I would suggest, however, that the Shari'a principle of apostasy, and notions of self-help and direct violent action common in early Muslim history, are significant factors in the Muslim reaction in this case.

For the sake of argument, it may be assumed that the book is extremely offensive to Muslims because it defames the Prophet Muhammad, his wives and several leading early Muslims. Furthermore, granted that freedom of expression is not absolute, one can conceive of restrictions on freedom of expression to safeguard other private and public interests. These considerations may justify calls for a book to be examined in accordance with the due process of law in a given country. When that is done, removal of offending passages may be required, whether with or without payment of compensation. One may even conceive of a ban on the circulation of a book if that is the only way to prevent significant harm to some private or public interest. But to call for the death of an author, even after a fair trial, is a serious violation of the human rights not only of the particular author, but of many others as well. The very existence of the crime of apostasy under Shari'a is a constant violation of freedoms of belief and expression of Muslims and non-Muslims alike.

In order to resolve human rights problems related directly or indirectly to the above noted principles of Shari'a, drastic Islamic reform is urgently needed. Otherwise, the superficial and temporary benefits of the so-called secularization of the Muslim world are likely to be lost, and extremely serious human rights problems will follow.

IV. Modern Shari'a and Human Rights

I have explained elsewhere the problems and prospects of Islamic law reform.[9] The basic point to emphasize in relation to an appropriate methodology of reform is an appreciation of the impact of historical context on the interpretation of the sources of Islam. In the same way that early Muslims interpreted the Qur'an and other sources in their context, contemporary Muslims must do the same at the present time.

Throughout its history, the understanding and implementation of Islam was influenced by the social and political realities of Muslim communities. In other words, the practical impact of the precepts of Islam was always and continues to be the result of human understanding of its scriptural sources in the particular historical context. While, as a Muslim, I believe that the Qur'an is divine, I also believe that there is no way of implementing divine texts without the intervention of human agency in terms of both interpretation and application. An appreciation of this elementary fact about all religious traditions, including Islam, is vital for a realistic and positive analysis of the relationship between religion and human rights.

The reform methodology I find particularly promising is the one proposed by the late Sudanese Muslim reformer, Ustadh Mahmoud Mohamed Taha.[10] According to this approach, the early process of abrogation (*naskh*) should now be reversed in order to implement the verses of the Qur'an which enjoin freedom of religion and equality between all human beings regardless of gender or religious faith.

Whether this or some other methodology of reform is employed today, the objective should be to guarantee all human rights under modern Islamic Shari'a in accordance with what might be called the principle of reciprocity. The basic premise of this principle, shared by all major religious traditions including Islam, is that a person should treat other persons in the same way that he or she wishes to be treated by them. In the Muslim context, this principle means that since Muslim men would claim human rights for themselves, they should guarantee the same rights to women and non-Muslims. Otherwise, Muslim men would not be justified in claiming human rights for themselves.

The restriction of this principle of reciprocity to Muslim men under Shari'a was justified by the historical context within which Muslim communities existed in the past. However, such restriction is neither morally justifiable nor politically possible at the present time. In the present global human community, extending the principle of reciprocity to all human beings has become vital for the very existence of mankind. The alternative is a constant state of hostility and antagonism incompatible with the realities of international relations and the political and economic interdependence of the modern world. Moreover, such hostility and antagonism will inevitably lead to war resulting in the total destruction of humankind through nuclear war. Seen in this light, human rights as rights to be accorded to every human being by virtue of being human have become a pragmatic necessity as well as a moral imperative. It is therefore my duty as a Muslim to understand and implement my own tradition in ways that are most conducive to the protection and promotion of human rights.

V. Conclusion

In the preceding discussion, I have distinguished between Islam and Shari'a in the sense that the latter is a particular interpretation of the former in a given historical context. Although I believe that a modern interpretation of Islam will produce a version of Shari'a which is capable of sustaining the full range of human rights and can accompany the further development of these rights, I also believe that the historical formulation of Shari'a is incapable of sustaining the most fundamental human rights today.

In my view, the fault is not that of the historical Shari'a as seen in its proper context. Rather, the fault is that of those contemporary Muslims who insist on implementing archaic concepts in radically transformed circumstances. The early Muslims have exercised their right and responsibility to interpret the divine sources of Islam in the light of their own historical context in order to produce a coherent and practicable system which achieved significant human rights improvements on its predecessors and contemporaries. It is the right and responsibility of contemporary Muslims to do the same in order to produce modern Islamic Shari'a for the present radically transformed context. Their failure to do so is the ultimate betrayal of their faith and total frustration of its divine purpose.

Notes

1. See, for example, verses 2:256, 3:64, 10:99 and 18:29 on freedom of religion; and verses 4:1 and 17:70 on the equal dignity of all human beings regardless of faith or gender. The Qur'an is cited here by chapter number followed by verse number in that chapter.

2. See, for example, verses 2:282 and 4:34 in relation to women, and 9:5 and 29 in relation to non-Muslims.

3. For the development of the concept of Shari'a and its subject-matter, see Fazlur Rahman, *Islam*, University of Chicago Press 1979, pp. 101–9.

4. See generally, A. An-Na'im, *Toward an Islamic Reformation*, Syracuse University Press 1989, especially chapters 4 and 7.

5. See 'Talak', in H. A. R. Gibb and J. H. Kramer (eds.), *Shorter Encyclopedia of Islam*, 1953, 564–7.

6. A. An-Na'im, 'The Rights of Women and International Law in the Muslim Context', *Whittier Law Review* 9, 1987, 491, 495.

7. A. An-Na'im, 'Religious Minorities under Islamic Law and the Limits of Cultural Relativism', *Human Rights Quarterly* 9, 1987, 1; A. An-Na'im, 'Religious Freedom in Egypt: Under the Shadow of the Dhimma System', in L. Swidler (ed.), *Religious Liberty and Human Rights in Nations and Religions*, Philadelphia: Ecumenical Press 1986, 43.

8. A. An-Na'im, 'The Islamic Law of Apostasy and its Modern Applicability: A Case from the Sudan', *Religion* 16, 1986, 197.

9. See An-Na'im, *Toward an Islamic Reformation* (n.4), chapter 3; and A. An-Na'im, 'Mahmud Muhammad Taha and the Crisis in Islamic Law Reform: Implications for Interreligious Relations', *Journal of Ecumenical Studies* 25, 1988, 1–21.

10. This approach is explained in detail in Mahmoud Mohamed Taha, *al-Risala al-Thaniya min al-Islam* (The Second Message of Islam), Omdurman, Sudan 1967. For an English translation of this book, see *The Second Message of Islam*, trans. Abdullahi A. An-Na'im, Syracuse University Press 1987.

The Foundations of Unity and Equality: A Hindu Understanding of Human Rights

Bithika Mukerji

I. A perspective on the contemporary emphasis on human rights

The hiatus which lies between what is factual and what is ideal, what 'is' and what 'ought to be', has been the focus of ethical concerns for all human societies. Human codes of conduct explicitly laid down or implicit in behavioural patterns have always guided primitive groups just as they now seek to determine our post-modern, permissive and a-moral societies. We have inherited quite a few engraven rules of conduct from ancient times; we have also learnt about the existence of admirable, near crime-free states, as for example that of the Inca chief Montezuma. Nomadic mores and tribal rules still follow a rationale which is supportive of these ways of life. In our own times we have witnessed with much appreciation the renewal and solidarity festivals of the gypsies of the world. They seem to possess an in-depth understanding of the human condition, its demand for justice among equals and a reaching out towards fulfilment hereafter.

It is useful to bear in mind not only the long history of the search for justice on earth but also the isolated instances of self-sufficient cultures which still adorn different parts of the world, because there is a tendency to think that an emphasis on moral codes is simultaneous with the coming into being of the great monotheistic religions, namely Judaism, Christianity and Islam. As a matter of fact a declared faith in one God does not seem to have added to the nobility of human behaviour. Truly, it is hoped that the tales of heresy-huntings, witch-burnings, infidel-killings and enforced conversions are stories of the past, now and for ever.

The last quarter of this century seems to be emerging as the era of human rights just as previous centuries were ages of colonization, religious expansionism and economic exploitation. These global tendencies have by and large originated from the West. It is in the fitness of things, perhaps, that the call for safeguarding human rights should also originate from the West. The West is so dynamic and possessed of such qualities of leadership that it must always seek to play a leading role in world affairs. It will not be far wrong to say that the sheer passivity of the East positively invited invasions in the past and even now encourages the tendencies of manipulative activities of alien powers.

A bird's-eye view of the past few centuries reveals an interesting phenomenon. The explosion of violence which brought to a halt the march of events in the West in the earlier part of the century seems to have transferred its area of influence to other parts of the world. The West, fearful of the consequences, has now eschewed violence, but not the means of violence, because that again is a matter of economic or political dominations. Violence now stalks the Third World because the means of violence are at hand. The will to violence, surely, follows upon the availability of the means of violence.

The reason for raising the question of the West and the rest of the world in this context is that insidious and infiltrating influences are more powerful and effective today than the forces of outright conquest in the name of king and religion. Unless one's attention is focussed on these facts, the question of human rights will remain less than lucid because by implying a denial of the right to self-determination, these policies legislate a denigration of human dignity at a deeper level.

In other words, if the upholding of human rights is undertaken as a step toward establishing equality amongst nations, then undeniably it is to be welcomed as a charter of freedom; whereas even a shadow of prescriptive laying down of laws would give it a touch of irony as being more akin to a penal code for policing the ethical standards of various nations. Realistically speaking, however, an ideal state of equality amongst nations lies in the future. In the meantime, the UNO Declaration on Human Rights is unquestionably a basic platform on which to build the house of future hopes.

II. Human rights derive from cultural patterns rather than religions

This may seem an opaque concept to begin with, but let us attempt a clarification of the issue. Traditions and cultural heritages are wider, deeper and more lasting than religious persuasions. Even revealed religions which may be called faiths by which men live and have their being are limited in their scope. By themselves they do not cut across barriers of time and space unless made to do so by fair means or otherwise. Cultures are more diffuse and pervasive; they establish inalienable and unalterable parameters for possibilities of transformations. We have come to realize the truth of this phenomenon by witnessing, for example, the experiences of the African nations. The quick transformation of authentic traditions into inauthentic pseudo-Western cultures has been a violation of human rights with far-reaching consequences. It is a violation because dozens of primitive cultures have been forced into the strait-jacket of modernity within a very short period of time with no regard to their inevitable destiny: the experience of rootlessness.

In retrospect, these problems are better understood to-day; it is also generally accepted that the question of human rights should be kept clear of religious dominations. It is a common contemporary phenomenon that people are only too ready to identify with ethnic traditions in opposition as it were to other common heritages. It will not be far wrong, therefore, to say that cultural patterns give shape and substance to human personalities. Our global existence, at this point in time, is a heterogeneous mixture of innumerable traditions ranging from the most primitive to the most sophisticated. It is even difficult to unravel the tangled skeins of many civilizations to see where the influence of one ends and another begins.

It is perhaps desirable that this should be so, and although demands of cultural forces should be recognized, it is also clear that the question of human rights can become significant only if we are going to move toward a homogeneous world ethic. The integration of individual traditional patterns into the larger whole of a world civilization can alone peacefully usher in the coming centuries. It remains to be seen whether this could be made into an enrichment with all components preserving their integral characteristics or whether the new culture is going to be a flat modern one without appreciation of its past heritages, or a looking forward to an overcoming of the present.

This brings us to the question which lies at the centre of human rights. It is self-evident that man-made laws, that is, the legal systems of the world, should be based upon equality. But (and this is an important 'but') this covers only a very small area of human behaviour. No laws can be framed, or rather implemented successfully, which bridge the lacunae between 'what one wants to do' and 'what one ought to do'. That everyone should be free to be themselves without curtailing the other's right to be free is the stumbling block for all lawgivers, ancient and modern. Freedom and equality are not compatible concepts. They can be held together only under specific conditions. All nations can examine their historical backgrounds to assess their own experiments in social organizations.

In India, the Hindu lawgivers are seen to address themselves to the task of organizing a society to uphold justice and establish peace and yet at the same time to be open to the quest for transcendence of the human condition itself. The Hindu tradition can only be understood as a way of life which tries constantly to keep the supreme human duty of self-enlightenment or, in the language of religion, God-realization, at the centre of attention. Further, it can be seen that it is here, in the region of the human quest for supreme felicity, that ethical concerns and religious commitments become united, because the fulfilment of the quest waits upon the grace of the Ultimate Being or Brahman.[1]

There is a remarkable piece of writing in the *Bhagavatapurana*, one of the most important texts for Hindus. The boy-prince Prahlada, who by virtue of his devotion to God is blessed and all-knowing as a seer, replies to a question put to him on the science of ethics. He says (in effect):

> I have no opinion on the subject of ethics. It is divisive, it teaches that men are superior or inferior (that is, one man to be kind or generous to another), or arrogance, that it is for man to uphold righteousness whereas men actually should try and contemplate and understand the indications of the pervasive quality of unity and equality obtaining in the world. One law, one rhythm upholds the entirety of creation, from the lowest to the highest: it is for man to support the eternal cosmic law of perfect harmony. Only the teaching of the one Reality (Brahman) alone can truly bring about goodness and justice and not any teaching which promotes differentiations (*Bhāgavatapurāṇa* I. 7.5–II).

III. The Hindu ideal of human life as the basis for social organization

Prahlada's words may be taken to be a summary of the Hindu tradition and its integral relationship to Hindu religious thought. The teaching of the One Reality (*Brahman*)[2] has been at the forefront of Hindu tradition from the times of the Vedas onwards. This teaching is based upon the concept that human nature is not only intrinsically connected with the entirety of nature, but also possesses the potentiality for transcending the natural order. For lack of space, it is not possible here to enter into philosophical explanations as to how the natural and the transcendental orders are held together; briefly, we may use the poetic language of the Upanishads to state that the *atman* (self) within human beings is the footprint of all-pervasive Brahman (*Bṛhadāraṇyakopaniṣad* 1.4.7). The *atman* in the guise of a human personality lives in oblivion of his true exalted status; he is to be guided toward a way of life which would help him to move onward on the path of recollection. Constant reminders of this gamut of values comprises the body of Hindu sacred literature, known as *Śāstra*. The main thrust of this corpus is to teach righteousness in life so that the yearning for transcendence should awaken and the miasma of forgetfulness be dispelled.

The word righteousness is a translation of the Sanskrit word *dharma*, a term with wide connotations. In order to explain what *dharma* is, it is necessary, however briefly, to go into the structuring of the human personality which is a microcosm analogous to the macrocosm of the world order. Although original to the ancient Sāmkhya-system,[3] the following theory of creation is also adopted by some other important and wide-ranging schools of thought and may be stated here in its most simplified form.

The world order is visualized as an unfolding into a complex structure from a simple state of equilibrium. This quiescent state is not static, but the stillness of many tensions held in perfect balance. The components termed qualities (*guṇa*) are three in number: 1. *sattva* (lightness, illumination, joy, buoyancy, etc.); 2. *rajas* (movement, excitement, pain, pleasure, etc.); 3. *tamas* (heaviness, sloth, opacity, etc.). This primeval material ground of creation is called *Prakṛti*. When the perfect balance is disturbed, as by, the glance of the Witness, the whole process of evolution is set into motion.

The Witness or the supreme spirit termed *Puruṣa* remains uninvolved and aloof (*Sāmkhya kasikā* 68). *Sattva*, being buoyant, is the first to evolve as cosmic intelligence. Thereafter a commingling of the three qualities in unequal degrees gives shape and substance to all things of the world, from the subtlest of mental processes to the grossest material. The nature of a thing is determined by the predominant quality in its composition: e.g. a stone is mostly *tamasic*, whereas light is very *sattvic*. It is the same with human nature. An apathetic, negative, slothful nature which resists activity has a predominance of *tamas* in his mental make-up; whereas an optimistic, cheerful, well-adjusted nature is predominantly *sattvic*. The quality of *rajas* denotes activity, mobility and stimulation.

Because of *rajas*, the mind suffers pain, excitement, as well as pleasurable enjoyments; it is the principle of involvement which establishes relationships.

All manner of drives to action or abstention from action arise out of the admixture of qualities which is the fabric of human nature. The importance of this analysis lies in the thought that the pattern of actions and behaviour in turn affects the level, or the composition, of qualities. This is the key to the mystery of the law of Karma. Human beings are born according to the propensities and predilections (*samskāra*) of past patterns of Karma, but are free not to continue in them. The inequality which obtains at birth may be changed by righteous action in life. Birth is therefore not a matter of accident or fortuitous circumstances. It is the result of past actions and a given platform for future ones.

All creatures automatically move toward the source of their being. This longing for 'a homecoming', as it were, is a subconscious process in the human being at its minimal strength, and a fully self-conscious yearning in a person who is aware of the highest duty enjoined on him or her as a moral protagonist in the world. The degree of realization of one's own true status as a creature, who is capable of working toward Enlightenment, is the foundation for the division into a caste system.

IV. The caste system as a social organization

The predominant qualities in the fabric of human nature decide a person's caste. The *brahmin* is truthful, honest, righteous, studious, abstemious, just, kind, generous, in fact the repository of all *sattvic* qualities. The *Kṣatriya* is brave, just, ready to give protection to others; the *Vaiśya* is astute, capable of husbanding the wealth of the community and stabilizing professions; the *Śūdra* is entrusted with the comprehensive task of serving the other castes.

The caste is mainly decided by birth, although it is stated clearly that anyone may forfeit his claim to a high caste or raise himself out of a lower caste by his actions in the world.[4] This particular type of social organization has to be seen in all its ramifications before it can be understood as a workable proposition. A few points are noted here for clarification:

1. Power and privileges are not coincident with the higher caste. The brahmins were poor and wholly dependent on charity, although they were accorded the highest place in society by virtue of their righteousness and learning. Their chief concern was the preservation of the Vedas by

constant study, recitation and the upholding of its precepts. Power was the privilege of the *Kṣatrīya* and wealth that of the *Vaiśya*. The *Śūdra* had no privilege but was entitled to the protection of all; his accountability was minimal whereas that of the brahmin was the maximum.

2. These divisions were fluid; it is explained in detail by Yudhiṣṭhira[5] that all men in effect are born equal because they have mixed qualities in their nature – their action in life will show up the caste to which they should belong.

3. A society which is constantly reiterating the teaching of the one Reality and man's ultimate destiny of realization of the self (*atman*) as Brahman could not err on the side of worldly possessions and enjoyment of temporal power. A further ballast to righteousness was provided by the ideal of the four stages of life. Each man's life was divided into four stages: first the stage of learning at the ashram of the guru; then, secondly, life in the world as a responsible citizen and householder; thirdly, the life of withdrawal from the world in company with one's wife; and lastly, renunciation of all attachments in order to begin on the quest for supreme knowledge.

4. A last point. According to this ethic, equality of opportunity was provided at a deeper level. The pursuit of self-enlightenment and its fulfilment was the birthright and privilege of all, irrespective of caste, sex or age. The enlightened seer was without any marks of distinction which gave position and status in the world. Thus it was ultimately the renunciate who could hold freedom and equality together in an ideal balance or could demonstrate by a living example the unity and equality of the entire created order.

The charge may be levelled that here a system of social order has been idealized out of all proportion to reality. On this, two points could be made. First, we are speaking here of ideals as far as human rights are concerned; second, the social order described above is fully substantiated and endorsed by the texts which have guided Hindu society for more than two thousand years. Leaving aside other books of equal authority, we may mention here only the epics, the *Ramayana* and the *Mahabharata*, the two unfailing sources of inspiration towards a righteous way of life. This is where the uniqueness of a tradition leaves its mark on the passage of time. These two texts are not outmoded, nor have they ceased to exercise the most profound effect on the Hindu community.

In summary, it may be said that a confluence of opposites marks the Hindu understanding of man's role in the world. The man of action is also subsequently the other-worldly renunciate. Time is very significant as a category of meaning as far as worldly activity is concerned. There is a time for everything, and everything must dwindle into insignificance at the moment of turning around towards the quest for timelessness.

V. The Hindu tradition in the light of contemporary influences

For centuries the Hindu tradition has been moving away little by little from the ancient ideals of renunciation and other-worldliness. The caste system is now a travesty of its past model. Instead of powers and privileges remaining diffuse and fluid, they are concentrated in one caste or another. The world is now recognized as the more important sphere of human engagement. The gap between the erstwhile ideal of human life and its reality is maximized, with the result that much of the teaching on righteous behaviour sounds meaningless. The talk of detachment and voluntary abdication of power sounds odd in a society given over to a consumer-orientated economy and party politics. The ancient Hindu tradition was shaken by the impact of alien forces.

The question remains whether out of this melting pot a synthesis of the old and the new will come forth soon enough to stabilize the contemporary social orders as they are emerging now. The rulers of India are very mindful of the movement towards the safeguarding of human rights. By following a policy of granting privileges and special opportunities in reverse order they are trying to usher in a classless society, or rather a society which will not be compartmentalized into higher or lower orders by birth.

From the point of view of the teaching incorporated in the *Mahābhārata* cited above, this may not be a moving away but an approximation to the true spirit of the Hindu tradition. It does after all emphasize the unity of the entire created order and equality in the possession of learning for truth. The modern age has given a secular interpretation to these ancient ideals. Perhaps the future will show if the Hindu tradition is able to continue in its upholding of renunciation as the ultimate aim of life in the midst of contemporary opposing influences.

Notes

1. *Kaṭhopaniṣad* I.11.22.
2. *Ṛg veda* 164.46.
3. See the *Samkhya-Kārikā* of Iśvara-Krsna.

4. The *Geeta*, Chapter XIV.

5. Yudhiṣṭhira, the hero of the *Mahābhārata*, answers searching questions about caste and its viability (*Mahābhārata* III. 177.18–32).

Select bibliography

Anirvana, *Buddhiyoga of the Gita and other Essays*, New Delhi: Biblia Impex Pvt Ltd, 1983

Bhagavad-gita

Bhartrihari Nitisatakam, tr. by P. P. Sharma, Allahabad: Ram Nasayana Lal 1959

S. K. Maitra, *The Ethics of the Hindus*, The University of Calcutta 1925

T. M. P. Mahadevan, *Invitation to Indian Philosophy*, New Delhi: Arnold-Heinemann Publishers Pvt Ltd 1974

H. Zimmer, *Philosophies of India*, Princeton University Press 1961

Human Rights in the Context of Global Problem-Solving: A Buddhist Perspective

Sulak Sivaraksa

1. New developments in Buddhism

To be honest and to begin by getting right to the point, I must state plainly that there is no serious contemporary Buddhist perspective for global problem-solving.

The World Fellowship of Buddhists, with its headquarters in Bangkok, has entirely avoided political, military and economic issues. It has not even dealt with environmental or human rights crises, nor has it promoted human co-operation. Members meet every few years to reaffirm how wonderful we Buddhists are: indeed, contemporary Buddhists seem to be interested only at national, local or denominational levels.

It is gratifying to learn, then, that the Asian Buddhist Conference for Peace (ABCP) is organizing a fourth international seminar on Buddhism and leadership for peace in August 1989 in Mongolia.

Other organizations, as well as the ABCP, have attempted to promote the development of a Buddhist approach to global problem-solving. For example, the United Nations University is currently supporting a sub-project on 'Buddhist Perceptions of Desirable Societies in the Future'.

At a meeting in Bangkok in 1986, a number of leading scholars and practising Buddhists came together to examine how religious thinkers and activists perceive the current human predicament. The framework of the meeting was divided into three main parts: 1. a diagnosis of current problems; 2. an examination of specifically Buddhist responses to these problems; and 3. a projection of how it might be possible to progress from the contemporary situation towards a more desirable society.

At the meeting, apathy, confusion and selfishness were identified as the main causes of the hopelessness that engulfs so many of the world's people, although these were not explicitly related to religion. At one point the slogan of the French revolution, 'Liberty, Equality and Fraternity', was discussed. Why did the Buddha not preach these values, rather than the Four Noble Truths: the existence of suffering, the causes of suffering, the cessation of suffering and the Noble Eightfold Path leading to the cessation of suffering?

The three values mentioned above are idealistic. The Buddha taught people to come to terms with, and surmount, the reality of human existence – the unavoidable problems of pain, loss, suffering, sickness and death. This approach was felt by many at the meeting in Bangkok to have a great deal to offer those engaged in solving contemporary global problems.

After the Bangkok meeting, the United Nations University set up a sub-committee which identified relevant issues to be tackled by Buddhists in order to move towards a more desirable society in the future regarding:

1. The individual and society in Buddhism
2. Universalism and particularism
3. Existing social practices which may lead to a more ideal society
4. Sangha, state and people
5. Buddhism and the evolution of society
6. Buddhist eschatology, millennialism and the Buddha land
7. Buddhist education
8. Buddhist approaches to war and violence
9. Science, technology and Buddhism
10. Women and family in Buddhism

Hopefully, the United Nations University will publish the relevant articles on these topics.

Recently, the United Nations University called for yet another meeting in Bangkok on the same theme of perceptions of desirable societies, but this time with respect to different religious and ethical systems. The conclusions were as follows:

We have reviewed briefly the position of different religious currents in terms of their beliefs and values regarding:
Welfare and development
Justice, equity and human rights
Peace, reconciliation and non-violence
Identity, authenticity and universality
It is important to realize that many of the divergencies existing among

religions are often complementary visions, which should not be seen as conflictual, but rather as differences which lead to deeper and more universal positions through a process of dialogue. It is crucial then that this process is guaranteed to take place by the religions, their institutions, and by society and the state.

These divergencies do not necessarily represent different religious beliefs but rather the positions of the religious thinkers or activists who choose either to be part of society, to accept its fundamental dynamics in order to transform it from within, or to stand outside it to develop a transcendental critical view of its values and institutions.

II. No Buddhist vision for present-day global problem-solving

Unlike Islam and Christianity, contemporary Buddhists have no vision for global problem-solving. This is partly due to the fact that prior to Western colonial expansion in the last century, Buddhism was divided into many schools, all of which were attached to national cultures and/or nation states, each with subdivisions into various denominations or sects.

Western Christianity, on the other hand, especially with its ties to the building of great empires such as the Roman and British empires, has evolved in such a way that the white man's burden includes caring for the world as a universality or catholicism. Although Protestantism was divided very much like Buddhism, it managed to pull together, with all its differences, to work on global issues, especially since the creation of the World Council of Churches.

The spread of Islam increased side by side with Arab commercial success and scientific knowledge, especially after the collapse of ancient Greek civilization. Although the Europeans replaced the Ottoman Empire in the nineteenth century, the rise of nationalism, pan-nationalism and economic success in the Middle East encouraged Muslims to have a more global outlook.

Although former Buddhist kingdoms in South and South-east Asia have regained their independence from the West, they have lost the Dhammic essence of their national identities. They have retained only state ceremonies which are often more feudal than Buddhistic. They blindly adhere to outmoded customs which are irrelevant to contemporary society.

Despite the fact that Siam was not subjugated politically, she was colonized intellectually, culturally and educationally. The effects of this type of colonization are almost impossible to reverse.

In East Asia, Buddhism lost much of its true essence to Confucianism or Shintoism, even before the arrival of Western influences.

The lofty Buddhist spirit remains in Asia only in small pockets of individual or local development where human needs are placed ahead of material or economic gains. At the national level, most people think only in terms of economic development. Hence, the rich get richer and the poor remain poor, or become poorer. This is true of nations and individuals. And of course, no one is happy. The present social-development systems lead to human-rights abuses, a widening gap between the rich and the poor, environmental degradation and the aggressive destruction of natural resources. Unfortunately, it seems that Buddhist development models have not been established, and overall, responses from the Buddhist communities have been insufficient to counter these negative elements.

Before attempting to deal with the above-mentioned issues, we ought to look into our Buddhist traditions to see whether such a global concern for social justice existed in the past, in order to apply it meaningfully in the present and the future.

III. Understanding the Buddhist myths of the great elect and the universal monarch

In my opinion, it is very worthwhile to examine the Buddhist mythological tradition regarding kingship and the universal monarch who ruled for the well-being of all, and to see how the myth was applied by Buddhist rulers of later generations.

The *Agganna Sutta* of the *Digha Nikaya* begins by portraying an ideal world of natural effortless existence. Ethereal, self-luminescent beings live in bliss and know no discrimination between polar opposites such as male and female, good and evil, rich and poor, ruler and subject. The earth itself is made of a delightful soft edible substance that looks like butter and is as sweet as honey.

Gradually, however, because of *karma* remaining from a previous world-cycle, this golden age comes to an end. During the long period of decline manifested in the world and its beings, greed, grasping, sex, theft, violence and murder are introduced. Finally, sheer anarchy prevails, and in order to put an end to it, the beings get together to select from among their ranks a king to rule over them and maintain order. This is the *Mahasommata*, the great elect, and in return for fulfilling his functions as a monarch, the beings each agree to pay him a portion of their rice.

Such is the myth of the first kingship. The record also relates the legend of the *Cakkravatin* (wheel-turning emperor) or universal monarch. A basic version of this appears in the *Cakkravatti Sihanada Sutta*, also of the *Digha Nikaya*.

This text, too, begins with a description of a golden age, the starting point of the world-cycle. During this time, beings had beautiful bodies, life-spans of eighty thousand years, and led wonderful effortless existences. This time, however, the *Cakkravartin*, Dalhanemi by name, is present from the beginning. He is, in fact, very much a part of the golden age, for his presence is instrumental in maintaining the paradisaical state. Because he knows what is good and rules through *Dhamma*, poverty, ill-will, violence, and wrongdoings do not exist in his domain.

Traditionally the *Cakkravartin* is portrayed as an extraordinary being. He is said to exhibit the thirty-two bodily marks of a Great Man (*Mahapurusa*) and to be endowed with the seven jewels or emblems of sovereignty, the most important of which is the wheel (*cakka*). In the *Sutta*, this magnificent wheel appears in mid-air before Dalhanemi at the beginning of his reign as a sign of his righteousness. It then leads him in a great cosmic conquest of the four continents.

It takes him East, South, West and North as far as the great oceans, and, where the wheel rolls, he encounters no resistance. The power of his *Dhamma*, symbolized by his wheel, the *Dhammacakka*, is such that local kings immediately submit to him.

Finally, his wheel leads him back to his capital at the centre of the world, and there it remains, miraculously suspended in mid-air over the royal palaces, as an emblem of sovereignty.

After many years of reigning in peace over a contented and prosperous empire, however, Dalhanemi's wheel of *Dhamma* begins to sink. This is a sign of the approaching end of his reign, according to the Buddhist law of change (*Anicca*), and when the wheel disappears altogether into the earth, the wise king entrusts his throne to his son and retires from this world to live as an ascetic in the forest.

It is important to note that the wheel of *Dhamma* is not automatically passed on from one *Cakkravartin* to the next. Dalhanemi's son must, in turn, prove worthy of his own wheel by calling forth with his own righteousness.

This fact sets the scene for the rest of the myth, which, like the story in the previous *Sutta*, traces the gradual degradation of this world and the beings in it.

After a long succession of Dalhanemi who are perfect *Cakkravartins*, there comes a king who fails to follow *Dhamma*, and for whom the wheel does not appear. Consequently, there is resistance to his rule. Friction develops; the people fail to prosper; the universal monarch fails to support them; and one thing leads to another, as it is stated in the *Sutta*: 'From not giving to the destitute, poverty grew rife; from poverty growing rife, stealing increased; from the spread of stealing, violence grew apace; from the growth of violence, the destruction of life became common; from the frequency of murder, both the life span of the beings and their beauty wasted away.'

The myth then goes on to trace the further decline in the quality and span of life, until a state of virtual anarchy is reached. In this respect, then, the myth of the *Cakkravartin* is quite similar to that of the great elect (*Mahasommata*).

Contrasting the two *Suttas*, one can draw different conclusions. In the former, the great elect is called upon only when the need for him arises. He functions as a stopgap against further anarchy, but the golden age itself requires and knows no king at all. In the latter, on the other hand, the ruler is a crucial part of the golden age. By his very presence and by his proper rule, he ensures a peaceful, prosperous, idyllic existence for all, and he will continue to do so as long as he is righteous enough to merit the wheel of *Dhamma*, that is, as long as he truly is a wheel-turning *Cakkravartin*.

The conclusion one can draw from these two myths is that neither myth stops at the golden age, but each goes on to describe, in no uncertain terms, what happens when a ruler does not live up to the ideal.

The suggestion is made, therefore, that there are really two possible types of rulers. One, a full-fledged *Cakkravartin*, is righteous and rules according to *Dhamma*, and so, like Dalhanemi, ensures a golden age. Indeed there is a saying by the Buddha in the *Anguttara Nikaya* stating that 'A universal monarch, a righteous and just king, relies on the *Dhamma*. Respecting, revering and honouring the *Dhamma*, with the *Dhamma* as his standard, he provides for the proper welfare and protection of his people.'

The other, perhaps not truly worthy of the title *Cakkravartin*, is not so righteous, and fails to rule according to *Dhamma*, and is responsible for a cosmic catastrophe, the degradation of the world.

These two myths have greatly influenced Buddhist monarchs in South and South-east Asia. However, in history, Emperor *Ashoka* of ancient India was perhaps the only one who could really be called a *Cakkravartin*, if one is to accept the prevailing world view. He was the 'universal monarch' who reigned as righteously as possible by extending his empire across almost all of the sub-continent.

The Sinhalese, Burmese and Siamese kings were not, in fact, *Cakkravartins*, but they all wished to imitate the great emperor, and tried their best, at least in theory, to be just and righteous.

In practice, however, it is questionable whether they actually 'respected, revered and honoured the *Dhamma*, while using the *Dhamma* as a standard, as a sign, as a sovereign, providing for the proper welfare and protection of the people'.

IV. The role of the *Sangha*

The result was that the institution of the *Sangha*, the holy community of brothers and sisters, was developed to teach *Dhamma* to the rulers and to facilitate communication between the rulers and the ruled.

Unlike the lay community, the *Sangha* reverses the process of degeneration of the human race described in the Buddhist creation myths: coercion is replaced by co-operation, private property by propertylessness, family and home by the community of androgynous wanderers, hierarchy by egalitarian democracy. The *Sangha* symbolizes the unification of means and ends in Buddhist philosophy. That is, the movement working for the resolution of conflict must itself embody a sane and peaceful process. The discipline of the early monastic *Sangha* was designed to channel expected conflicts of interest among the monks and nuns into processes of peaceful democratic resolution. In order to spread peace and stability in their societies, the monastic *Sangha* sought to establish moral hegemony over the state, to guide their societies with a code of non-violent ethics in the interest of social welfare.

Since the passing away of the Buddha, some 2530 years ago, the historical *Sangha*, however, has been divided vertically and horizontally by cultural, economic and political alliances. Sectors of the *Sangha* in many different countries became dependent on state patronage for their growing communities. With the growth of monastic wealth and land-holding came the integration of the *Sangha* into society as a priest-class of teachers, ritual performers, and chanters of magic formulas – a sector of the land-owning élite with its own selfish interests and tremendous cultural power.

With the centralization of the *Sangha* and the formation of a hierarchy came increasing élitism and state control, so that instead of applying the ethics of non-violence to the state, a part of the *Sangha* was increasingly called upon to rationalize violence and injustice.

On the other hand, at the base of society, frequently impoverished and poorly educated, there have always been propertyless and familyless radical clergy who maintain the critical perspective of the Buddha. To this day, scattered communities of Buddhists continue in a radical disregard, and sometimes fiery condemnation, of the official 'State Buddhisms' – their élite hierarchical structures and their legacies of secular accommodation and corruption.

In looking to the future of humanity it is therefore necessary to look back and transfer the state and its élites, with their natural tendency towards acquisitive conflict, under the hegemony of the popular institutions that embody the process of non-violent, democratic, conflict resolution. In traditional Buddhist terms, the king should always be under the influence of the *Sangha*, and not vice versa.

I feel it is imperative that those of us who are lay intellectuals should support the radical clergy in maintaining this critical perspective of the Buddha. We should whole-heartedly support the *Sangha* in its efforts to lead the local communities towards self-reliance and away from domination by élites or their consumerism.

Indeed, many of the local and agrarian societies still have non-violent means of livelihood and respect for each individual as well as for animals, trees, rivers and mountains.

Although the government and multi-national corporations have introduced various technological 'advances' and chemical fertilizers and have advertised to make villagers turn away from their traditional ways of life and opt for jeans, coca-cola and fast food as well as worship of the state and its warlike apparatus, their efforts have been successfully countered by those of the critical *Sangha*. Some of them have even reintroduced meditation practices for farmers, established rice banks and buffalo banks which are owned by the communities and benefit them, rather than the commercial banks which link with international enterprises at the expense of the local population.

V. The importance of a socially engaged spirituality

We should strengthen and extend the liberation potential within the Buddhist tradition to allow each local community to gain a global perspective making each aware of global problems, especially the suffering of the poor. If more people were conscious of the problem, it could be solved more efficiently.

We should also promote exchange and learning between Buddhists and non-Buddhists in order that they can co-operate meaningfully in a common struggle against the oppressive social forces that cause suffering.

We should also try to enable peasants, fishermen, industrial workers, women and all oppressed factions in any country to discover their faith and the roots of their culture and draw inspiration and sustenance from them.

Unfortunately, development in the past has ignored this vital source of human values. Indeed, activists, even those of agnostic tendency, should be open to the liberative dimensions of religions and cultures. Of course, many activists are anti-religious; perhaps against certain dogmas, forms, ceremonies or establishments. However, perhaps buddhism with a small 'b' could help them to discover, develop and strengthen a secular spirituality of struggle that does not make overt references to one specific tradition, but nourishes individuals for greater authenticity.

For many of us who want to solve global problems, on one hand there is the prevalent social-engineering mentality which assumes that personal virtue can be more or less conditioned by a radical restructuring of society. The opposite view is that radical social improvement is wholly dependent upon personal and spiritual change and changes in life-style. But a growing number of spiritually-minded people recognize that the 'inner' work is massively discouraged by the social conditions which are the consequence of individual delusion and fear. Thus, an American Zen Buddhist poet and activist, Gary Snyder, remarks that the so-called 'free world' has become economically dependent on a fantastic system of greed that cannot be fulfilled, sexual desire which cannot be satiated, and a hate which has no outlet, except against oneself. Under these conditions, the odds are heavily against a spiritual life-style, especially when one lives in an affluent society in the West. Yet the so-called 'socialist societies' have, almost without exception, wanted to join the so-called 'free world'.

Therefore, this vicious circle must be broken socially as well as personally – a socially engaged spirituality is needed.

Social activism in the past has been mostly preoccupied with what is 'out there'. Opening up to what is 'in here' and sharing it with others can bring great relief, but it also brings a disconcerting awareness of how much 'I' need *my* busyness, *our* certainties or rationalizations and *their* malevolence. Just to maintain awareness of the boredom, frustration, indifference, anger, hostility and triumphalism experienced by the activist without being carried away or cast down is an invaluable spiritual practice. But this is only possible if there is an adequate balance of daily meditation and periodic retreat, by also being aware of social ills outside ourselves.

These practices slowly dissolve the self-need that feeds on hope, setting us free to do just what the situation demands of us.

Through deepening awareness comes acceptance, and through acceptance comes a seemingly miraculous generosity of spirit and empowerment
for the work that compassion requires of us. We can even take ourselves
less seriously. With this critical self-awareness, we can genuinely understand and respect others of diverse religions and beliefs. We can even join
hands with them humbly and knowingly in trying to develop our spaceship
earth to be peaceful and just.

VI. A new interpretation of the Buddhist concept of interrelated-ness and the application of the Five Precepts to the con-temporary situation

Buddhism, through its insistence on the interrelatedness of all life, its
teachings of compassion for all beings, its non-violence, and its caring for
all of existence, has been leading some contemporary Buddhists to broader
and deeper interpretations of the relationship between social, environmental, racial and sexual justice and peace.

In this area, we should be inspired by examples of such movements as
that of Ven. Bhikkhu Buddhadasa and his Garden of Liberation in Siam,
not to mention the meditation practices of Ven. Phra Ajan Cha Subaddho
and the scholarly work of Ven. Phra Debvedi (Payutto) which inspired not
only Thai but foreign monks like Ven. Sumedho to carry the Buddhist
message with social concern to Europe, North America, Australia and
New Zealand. However, in this paper, I want to concentrate on one
Vietnamese monk, Thich Nhat Hanh, who teaches us to pay close
attention to the minute particulars in our actions, as well as to the giant web
of all life.

He particularly stresses non-dualism in his teachings, and speaks of
being peace in the moments in one's own life, as part of making peace in the
world. He stresses the continuity of inner and outer, calling the world our
'large self', and asks us to become it actively and to care for it.

His Tiep Hien order, created in Vietnam during the war, is in the lineage
of the Zen school of Lin Chi. It is a form of engaged Buddhism in daily life,
in society. The best translation of Tiep Hien, according to Thich Nhat
Hanh, is the 'Order of Interbeing', which he explains in this way: 'I am,
therefore you are. You are, therefore I am. That is the meaning of the word
interbeing. We inter-are.'

The Order of Interbeing is designed explicitly to address social justice
and peace issues, sensitizing the participant to test his/her behaviour in
relation to the needs of the larger community, while freeing him/her from

limiting patterns. Even the way we take refuge in the Triple Gems is explained simply and beautifully:

> I take refuge in the Buddha,
> the one who shows me the way in this life,
> *Namo Buddhaya*

> I take refuge in the Dharma,
> the way of understanding,
> and love,
> *Namo Dharmaya*

> I take refuge in the Sangha;
> the community of mindful harmony,
> *Namo Sanghaya*

Thich Nhat Hanh revised the traditional Five Precepts to address issues of mind, speech and body:

First, do not kill. Do not let others kill. Find whatever means possible to protect life. Do not live with a vocation that is harmful to humans and nature.

Second, do not steal. Possess nothing that should belong to others. Respect the property of others, but prevent others from enriching themselves from human sufferings and the sufferings of other species on earth.

Third, sexual expression should not take place without love and commitment. Be fully aware of the sufferings you may cause others as a result of your misconduct. To preserve the happiness of yourself and others, respect the rights and commitments of others.

Fourth, do not say untruthful things. Do not spread news that you do not know to be certain. Do not criticize or condemn things that you are unsure of. Do not utter words that cause division and hatred, that can create discord and cause the family or the community to break. All efforts should be made to reconcile and resolve all conflicts.

Fifth, do not use alcohol and any other intoxicants. Be aware that your fine body has been transmitted to you by several previous generations and your parents. Destroying your body with alcohol and other intoxicants is to betray your ancestors, your parents and also to betray the future generations.

These precepts create a consciousness of, and a precedent for, social justice and peace work, grounded firmly in Buddhist principles in our individual beings and in our practice of mindfulness. As well, Thich Nhat Hahn often reminds us:

> Do not lose yourself in dispersion and in your surroundings. Learn to practise breathing in order to regain composure of body and mind, to practise mindfulness, and to develop concentration and understanding.

These guiding statements achieve an integration of the traditional five precepts with elements of the Noble Eightfold Path. I believe Thich Nhat Hanh's decision to elaborate on the traditional precepts came from his observation that one can interpret these to encourage a withdrawal from the world, a passivity in the face of war and injustice, a separation of oneself from the common lot of humanity. In rewriting the precepts, he is countering that tendency. In directing us to focus on our interconnection with other beings, he is asking us to experience the continuity between the inner and the outer world, to act in collaboration, in mutuality with others in the dynamic unfolding of the truth that nurtures justice and creates peace.

VII. International network of engaged Buddhists: a hopeful beginning for global problem-solving?

Some of us are trying to meet this challenge, and I hope what some of us are trying to do in connecting our being peace within to the outside world engagingly and mindfully will contribute to a better world, with social justice, non-violence and with ecological balance – the Middle Way for each and for society at large, to live in harmony with one another and with nature.

Groups of young people in the West who believe in these principles and who try to act accordingly have established chapters of the Buddhist Peace Fellowship in the USA, UK and Australia.

On top of that, some of us have also tried to meet with like-minded fellow Buddhists in order to solve global problems concretely, taking some relevant issues of social justice which are near and dear to us, which we feel we could tackle individually and collectively with good friends (*kalayama-mitta*) in other countries and cultures. Thus, last February, in a small city outside Bangkok, some forty-five Buddhists from all over the world, including a representative from the ABCP, met:

1. To identify urgent social problems which exist in one's own country as well as those affecting other Buddhist communities.
2. To explore the ways in which participants could co-operate in acting on these issues.
3. To establish a network among engaged Buddhists on a global level.

They set up four working groups to explore different issues:

1. Education
2. Women's issues
3. Human rights
4. Spirituality and activism

It is not appropriate to go into the details of this meeting here. However, since some Buddhists have become aware of the shortcomings of the World Fellowship of Buddhists and similar organizations, they are now determined to set up the International Network of Engaged Buddhists, with the following objective:

1. To promote understanding between Buddhist countries and various Buddhist sects.
2. To facilitate and engage in solving problems in various countries.
3. To help bring the perspective of engaged Buddhism to bear in working on these problems.
4. To act as a clearing house of information on existing engaged Buddhist (and relevant non-Buddhist) groups and activities, and aid in the co-ordination of efforts wherever possible.

They will initially involve groups and individuals working in the following areas:

1. Alternative education and spiritual training
2. Peace activism
3. Human rights
4. Women's issues
5. Ecology
6. Family concerns
7. Rural development
8. Alternative economics
9. Communication
10. Concerns of monks and nuns

This may be expanded in the future.

I trust that this newly-established network will collaborate meaningfully with other religious organizations of similar ecumenical outlook in applying spiritual values to global problem-solving.

III · Possibilities for the Future

World Religions, Human Rights and the Humanum

Report on a Symposium in Paris

Karl-Josef Kuschel

Paris, 1989. It is not possible to travel to the French capital at present without being reminded of the French Revolution which took place there 200 years ago. And one cannot think of the French Revolution without remembering the epoch-making declaration of human rights which was adopted and was accepted by the King(!) in the early stages of the Revolution, before the Reign of Terror that is. And one cannot speak of this declaration of human rights without feeling shame as a Christian. After almost 2000 years of Christianity 'natural and lasting human rights' were once and for all codified – without the Christian churches, indeed against them. Any kind of privilege or even discrimination because of religious convictions was rigorously rejected. In the famous Article 10 of the French Declaration of the Rights of Man of August 1789 it is stressed: No one should be harrassed for his opinions, even religious opinions, provided that they do not disturb public order as established by law.

I. The changed situation

It took a long time, more than 150 years, before another epoch-making declaration of human rights could be adopted. On 10 December 1948 the General Assembly of the United Nations proclaimed in Article 1: 'All human beings are born free and equal in dignity and rights. They are endowed with reason and conscience and should act towards one another in a spirit of brotherhood.' And on religion? On religion Article 18 now says more positively and in more detail: 'Everyone has the right to freedom of thought, conscience and religion; this right includes freedom to change his religion or belief, and freedom, either alone or in community with others and in public or private, to manifest his religion or belief in teaching, practice, worship and observance.'

Religion, its teaching and practice, its proclamation and exercise – protected by a secular declaration on 'natural and inalienable human rights'! The freedom of religion – the concern therefore of a secular human rights movement. But in reverse? Secular human rights the concern also of religion? Freedom of religion, freedom of conscience, freedom of opinion, freedom of assembly – the affair of the church? The question does not arise by chance. In 1791 Pope Pius VI had expressly disapproved of the French Revolution's Declaration of the Rights of Man (particularly with regard to religious freedom). He was followed in this by his successors Gregory XVI and Pius IX. In the infamous Syllabus of 1864 Pius IX rejected the view that the 'Catholic religion' no longer had the status of a 'unique religion' and that the 'other cults' were no longer excluded.

Today the situation seems to have fundamentally changed, in two respects.

First: within Christianity a process can be discerned, in the twentieth century at the latest, of perceiving and recognizing the Christian roots of secular human rights movements, as well as participating in the declaration of human rights for genuinely Christian reasons. The Catholic Church, too, has, with the declaration of religious freedom at the Second Vatican Council, achieved an epoch-making breakthrough. Human rights are no longer understood as rivals to a specifically Christian image of humanity, but as its inheritance and concrete form. Human rights can, on the contrary, find a deeper justification from the specifically Christian approach and can be propagated in a generally more binding manner.

Secondly: the global interconnection of ever more areas of human existence (politics, economics, transport, environment) has, in the second half of the twentieth century at the latest, brought about incalculable consequences for relationships among the great world religions. A global ecumenical consciousness has awoken not only within Christianity but also between religions. The co-existence of human beings of different religious convictions is becoming ever less abstract; indeed, in many countries in the world it is becoming a concrete daily task. Jews, Muslims, Hindus and Confucians often live together with Christians in one and the same town. A poly-religious world has evolved out of a poly-centric one. This development creates a new ecumenical situation whose challenge we must take into account.

For it is indeed a fact that each of the great religions has its own completely separate, different forms of legitimation and its own concepts. Each of the great religions relies on different bearers of revelation (a person, a book, a law) or has developed different concepts and practices. Libraries have been written to bring out these structural and conceptual differences or indeed incompatibilities.

But it is also a fact that, however different the structure and concept of the various world religions may be, members of different religions can live together without jeopardizing each other's right to exist. Members of different religions can live in a society and together help to build it up and maintain it. There must therefore be something which unites religions to which, regardless of their different structures and concepts, they can subscribe. For living together is only possible when one subscribes to rules of law. But rules of law are founded on values for whose protection and promotion they are created. Values, however, presuppose ethics, or, better put and in more concrete terms, a consensus in ethically founded forms of behaviour, a consensus in values and convictions which are ultimately founded on the fact that each possesses a lasting value and an inalienable dignity. There must therefore be something among religions which they can accept without coming into conflict with themselves. The following question is therefore not only legitimate but, in the face of a growing world society, of the highest importance in political-practical terms: are there, within the individual religions, values for a practical code of behaviour which would recur in other religions? Is there such a thing as a universal ethic of humankind? Are there fundamental convictions, guiding values and basic commandments to which human beings of various religions can subscribe each out of his or her own tradition? After all, was not the United Nations Declaration of Human Rights also signed by states which are totally of a Muslim, Buddhist, Hindu or Confucian stamp?

II. The search for an ethic of humankind

This is the exact starting point of a colloquium which took place in Paris from 8–10 February 1989. It was held at the invitation of the Goethe-Institute in Paris and UNESCO, whose German representatives had taken overall charge at this colloquium. The commitment of UNESCO to the matter of world religions is completely consistent. We know with this organization that changes in the direction of more 'brotherhood' among nations, of a greater realization of human rights and responsibility for peace, can only succeed with these religions and not against them. These are religions which, in the countries of Africa and Asia and of the Near and Middle East, have a totally different influence on people from that in post-Enlightenment Europe. The present Director-General of UNESCO, Frederico Mayor, also emphasized in his opening address the importance of world religions for the UNESCO programme 'Education for Human Rights'. The perception of the differences between religions, he said, did not exclude the search for uniform values; indeed, the international community could not exist without common values. Unity *in* diversity, UNESCO's programmatic slogan, itself presupposed a consciousness of such common features.

A core paper by the ecumenical theologian Hans Küng from Tübingen formed the basis of the conference. He was the real guiding spirit of this symposium. Not only was its ecumenical work with world religions over the last ten years the catalyst for this event, but he had also been requested to nominate the representatives of the various world religions who could participate in such a dialogue. So, the Jewish representative was the American Eugene B. Borowitz, the Muslim was the Paris historian Muhammed Arkoun, the Hindu the Indian Professor of Religious Studies Bithika Mukerji from the University of Benares, the Buddhist representative the philosopher Masao Abe from the University of Kyoto (Japan), and finally the Confucian the philosopher Liu Shu Hsien from the Chinese University in Hong Kong.

All had brought with them papers to accompany Küng's core paper which had the general title of 'No world peace without religious peace. An ecumenical path between being fanatical for the truth and forgetting the truth'. In it Küng had taken the following as his starting points:

1. Religions were, in the course of their history, not only bringers of peace but also bringers of strife. They not infrequently brought a dimension of fanatacism to political, racial, cultural or ethnic antagonisms, a fanatacism which was ready to walk in God's name across hetacombs of corpses.

2. The fanatacism and irreconcilability of religions were connected above all with the question of truth. In short, every religion has considered itself to be the true religion either in an exclusive way (as pre-eminently the prophetic religions of Semitic origin) or in an inclusive way (as pre-eminently the mystic religions of Indian origin) and in doing so shuts out the others, ignores them or integrates them.

3. A conversation between religions on the question of truth is only

promising if every religion is ready to exercise voluntary self-criticism. A dialogue between religions presupposes an awareness that the boundary between true and false no longer runs between my religion and any others, but also within my own religion.

4. Every religion has, first of all, its own criteria of judgment as to what is true or false, as for example the criterion for what is original and canonical. In almost all religions the awareness has remained alive that the origins were once more authentic, more pure, 'more true' than what was later made of them. So reformers in all religions have constantly gone back to the origins and critically measured their respective reality by that criterion. The same goes also for the 'binding' canonical writings which, compared to the oral or written traditions of later centuries, retained their liberating function as criteria in many religions.

5. Going beyond these internal criteria: are there not also judgmental criteria of a general, ethical kind, according to which the truth or falseness of the respective religions can and must be judged? So, among the specifically internal religious criteria, are there not also external ecumenical criteria which can and must be applied to every religion?

III. The Humanum as a criterion of truth?

And so we come back to the starting point of our considerations. And this point is decisive. For Küng's paper also explodes when he put forward the following thesis: the *humanum*, that is to say, the truly human, is (together with the internal criteria of truth) an additional criterion of truth for religions. For only a religion which promotes humanity can be a true and good religion. True humanity is the prerequisite of true religion! Humanity is therefore a minimum demand on all religions, which means conversely: in so far as a religion spreads inhumanity, in so far as it impedes human beings' sense of identity, meaning and value, it is a false and bad religion.

This thesis met with misunderstanding and dissent in the other papers and in discussions at the symposium. Religion, it was objected, is surely always the relation of the human being to the Absolute. Could the *humanum* in isolation function as a judgment on religions which after all were founded on the Absolute? Was this not building a kind of 'superstructure' over concrete religions, a structure according to which religions were now to be judged and condemned? Was not the *humanum* – the result of European humanism influenced by Christianity – a typically Western criterion which in no way applied to the Eastern religions? Was

not the *humanum* as an ecumenically common criterion by its very nature
too vague to be binding on religions?

The misunderstandings were clarified in the course of conversations.
For, already in his core paper, Küng had placed a maximum criterion
beside his minimum one. True religion is the fulfilment of true humanity!
Religion is the optimal prerequisite for the realization of the human. There
has to be religion (as a maximum criterion) if there is to be humanity as an
unconditional and universal obligation. So, there is a basic dialectical
connection between religion and humanity. This provided the basis for an
emerging consensus amongst the representatives of the various religions as
the conference proceeded:

1. No representative accepted an 'autonomous *humanum*' as a superstructure over concrete religions. Each affirmed that the *humanum* had to
be grounded in the Absolute (however that was understood among religions). The criterion of the *humanum* lost its vagueness the moment one
had to complain about specific violations of humanity.

2. All representatives accepted self-criticism as a presupposition of
dialogue between religions. All representatives conceded that, in the name
of their religion, human dignity and human rights were still being abused,
violence and hatred still being stirred up, peace being made impossible and
destruction being caused. All agreed that it was precisely in the religions
that there was a need for action to educate human beings to humanity and
the capability for peace. No one contradicted the slogan of the whole
symposium: 'No world peace without religious peace'.

3. All representatives of the great world religions affirmed principally
the possibility of basing humanity on each religion's own tradition. Here
humanity was not seen as an 'invention' of the West. On the contrary. The
Jewish representative, E. B. Borowitz, said: 'Judaism has, without doubt,
a classic religious basis for agreeing to a universal ethical reality.'
Mohammed Arkoun spoke of the Qur'an as the 'ideal code of human rights'
and pointed to the most recent official Muslim declaration of human rights
in 1988. The Hindu representative spoke of a close connection between
morality and religion and of the need to resist the self-destructive forces of
the world. Even the Buddhist said that recognizing the transanthropocen-
tric and cosmological dimension of human beings in Buddhism did not
exclude or render impossible their specific importance as human beings in
the universe. It was the very wisdom of Buddhism with its strong emphasis
on compassion which implied 'the recognition and acceptance of every man
and woman in their diversity and in their uniqueness'. And it was the
Confucian who went furthest, being able to state emphatically that, from

the great humanistic tradition of Confucianism, 'the search for ecumenical criteria presents no problem for the Confucian tradition. *The humanum* has always been the central concern of Confucianism.'

IV. Tasks for the future

This threefold consensus is of the greatest importance for a future discussion among world religions on basic questions of human ethical values. What remains to be done for the future? The future should fall under the keyword 'concretion' – in three respects.

1. *A concrete universal basic ethic*. It would be of the greatest importance for the history of mankind if something like a code of 'Ten Commandments' could be arrived at, to which members of all religions could agree to. The demand for a universal basic ethic values within the one universal global society is more urgent than ever, if the world is not to fall apart into areas in which different ethical codes of action are valid.

2. *Ethical concretization*. The investigations and discussions between religions should be extended as far the consensus on human rights and human dignity goes in material ethical questions. Large ethical problem areas (from genetics to the atom and ecology) are a common challenge to all world religions. Basic ethical principles and the concrete universal ethic would therefore have to be applied to a particular situation.

3. *Political concretization*. It was important that at this colloquium theologians and specialists in religion were able to speak for once among themselves and with each other without immediately getting caught up in complicated political questions. It cannot, however, be overlooked that the practice of human rights, whether in Christian, Buddhist, Hindu or Confucian countries, often makes a mockery of the *theory* of human rights.

The Goethe Institute was therefore well advised to follow the theological human rights colloquium with a political one. Here, representatives from various countries showed in frightening clarity how in many countries in this world, human rights and human dignity are still being trampled on and how little religions can still achieve in concrete political praxis in opposing this. Theological theory and political praxis must therefore be even more emphatically reconciled in future. That religions should, on a mass basis, become champions and guardians of human rights throughout the world: therein lay the main consensus, the political worth of which has still to be proved. But what was it the German dramatist Bert Brecht said: 'Truth? Truth is always also concrete!'

Translated by Gordon Wood

Towards a World Ethic of World Religions

Fundamental questions of present-day ethics in a global context

Hans Küng

The danger of a vacuum in meaning, values and norms

Why should a human being do good and not evil? Elementary questions are often the most difficult of all – and today such questions are no longer only for the 'permissive' West. Much in terms of customs, laws and traditions that was taken for granted throughout the centuries, because it was safeguarded by religious authority, is no longer a matter of course anywhere in the world. One might ask concretely in respect of evil:

Why should human beings not deceive, cheat and rob their fellow human beings if this is to their advantage and they have no fear of discovery and punishment in a particular case?

Why should the politician resist corruption if he can be sure of the discretion of his financial backers?

Why should the businessman limit his concern for profit if greed and the 'get rich' slogan are publicly preached without any moral scruples?

Why should the embryo researcher not develop a commercial reproductive technique which manufactures guaranteed perfect embryos and casts the rejects into the rubbish bin?

But the question is not only directed at the individual: why should a people, a race, a religion, if they have at their disposal the necessary instruments of power, not hate and bully and, if that is their concern, even exile and liquidate a minority that is different and believes something different, an 'alien' minority.

Or one might ask in respect of good:

Why should human beings always be friendly, gentle, even helpful to other human beings? Why should a young person in particular renounce the use of force and opt in principle for non-violence?

Why should the entrepreneur or the banker, even if no one is supervising, behave with unconditional correctness? Why should the trade union official, even if it were to damage his career, not only fight for his own organization but also for the general good?

Why, for the scientist and for a doctor working on transplantation, should a human being, in experiment and therapy, never be the object of commercialization and industrialization (the embryo already as a proprietary article and object of trade), but always a legal subject and an end?

But the question must also be put in quite general terms: why should one people, or one race, or one religion show tolerance, respect or even reverence towards another? Why should those who wield power among the nations and religions commit themselves in every case to peace and never to war?

So, once again, the fundamental question: why should human beings – understood as individuals, groups, nations, religions – why should they behave in a humane way, a truly humane way, that is, with humanity? And why should they do this unconditionally, that is, in every case? That is the basic question in every system of ethics, that is to say, in every doctrine (philosophical or theological) of values and norms which should guide our decisions.

Such fundamental questions are often asked today, often even by young people in a quite open and radical manner, at least in our Western industrial societies where achievement and consumerism are the norm. How many of them today no longer know what the basic options are which should help them make the daily minor or major decisions in their lives, what preferences they should follow, what priorities they should set themselves, and which role-models they should choose. The reason is that the old authorities and traditions that gave them their orientation are no longer valid. Through the media, human beings are being showered with a wealth of fleeting images which, in both the private and the public sphere, more often than not fail to provide orientation. For a long time it has been no secret that, at the most widely varying social levels, as well as at all age levels, a clear crisis of orientation is rife, in spite of, or because of, all this excess of information. This crisis of orientation is as much connected with drug addiction and crime amongst young people as with the most recent scandals in the world of politics, the economy, unions and society. The scale of these scandals, at least in Germany and Japan, is unprecedented.

And since the official ideology of the Communist state is now, to a large extent, bankrupt in the Eastern states – those within both the Soviet and Chinese spheres of influence – and the Stalinist party discipline has also been undermined, where it has not yet collapsed with increasing glasnost and perestroika, we shall ultimately see exactly the same signs of a lack of orientation, not only in the Soviet Union but also in Catholic Poland (a large number of Poles who have so far come to the West already no longer practise their belief). But for the 'capitalist' countries as well as the 'socialist' ones, it is not just a question here of the private problems of the individual psyche and a healthy soul, but rather a political issue of the very highest order. It must be of concern to all those in positions of responsibility in state, church and society, when an increasing number of people, and particularly the young, are virtually facing a vacuum in meaning, values and norms. Total withdrawal from politics, football hooliganism and alcoholism in the 1980s are no less disturbing than political anti-authoritarianism, revolutionary activity, violent protest, even terrorism in the late 1960s and the 1970s.

And as far as the countries between the blocs are concerned, can one – in view of these 'side-effects' of Western modernization and secularization which are constantly increasing in India, South-East Asia, Arab countries and black Africa – can one not understand the fierce reproaches levelled at 'the West', namely that it is destroying the old ways of life, concepts of value and their resultant ways of behaviour, without putting new ones in their place? What authority, it is asked, is now valid in family, state and society for all those sons and daughters who have been emancipated or 'contaminated' by Western style, who now, in line with the 'capitalist ethic', only make money, achieve promotion and seek personal enjoyment, an enjoyment whenever possible without remorse?

Democracy without morality?

In fact, there is widespread criticism on the part of non-Western countries that while the West has given the world a great deal, it has not been all good. The West has given:

> *science*, but no wisdom in order to prevent the misuse of scientific research (why not also consider the industrial production of human matter in Japan?);

technology, but no spiritual energy to bring the unforeseen risks of a highly efficient, major technology under control (why not also work on atom bombs in India and Pakistan instead of putting a stop to the mass poverty?);

industry, but no ecology to combat the ever-expanding economy (why not cut down the Brazilian tropical rain forest by the square kilometre?);

democracy, but no morality which could counteract the huge power interests of the various men of power and the power groups (but what can one do to combat the Colombian drug cartel, the corruption in the Indian Congress Party, in the Japanese National Liberal Party or in Mobutu's Zaire?).

So the great achievements of the West are viewed, especially by the intellectual élite of Third-World countries, with increasing distrust: what is modern democracy's attitude to morality? It ought to be evident that here we have a fundamental problem of Western democracy on which we should not moralize self-righteously but rather reflect self-critically. For in the way in which it sees itself the liberal-democratic state – in contrast to the authoritarian-clerical state or the modern totalitarian state – must be ideologically neutral: that is to say, it must tolerate different religions and confessions, philosophies and ideologies. It was without doubt a huge step forward in human history that the democratic state must, according to its constitution, respect, protect and further freedom of conscience and religion, freedom of the press and right of assembly, everything that can be counted as modern human rights. But for all that, the state cannot decree precisely what meaning life should have and how it should be lived; it cannot prescribe any supreme values and ultimate norms, if it does not wish to damage its ideological neutrality.

Here, therefore, lies the root of the dilemma of every modern democratic state (be it in Europe, America, India or Japan): it is at the same time dependent on what it cannot prescribe by law. For here too there is now general agreement: without a minimal basic consensus on particular values, norms and attitudes there is no possibility, either in a smaller or a larger community, of living together in a manner which befits human dignity, nor can a modern democracy function without that. Indeed, as for example the Weimar Republic of 1919–1933 proved – it will sink into chaos or into dictatorship.

The necessary basic consensus

What does a minimal basic consensus mean? I will clarify that with a few points:

> The *inner peace* of a smaller or a larger community presupposes the agreement that people want to resolve social conflicts without violence.
>
> *Economic and legal rules* presuppose that people definitely want to hold on to a particular rule and laws.
>
> *Institutions* which sustain these rules, but which are subject to constant historical change, presuppose that the people's assent to the rules is always being renewed, at least tacitly.

What, however, if exactly the opposite happens in the technological state grown abstract and incalculable, and people react with terror in the ideological conflicts? What if crass Machiavellianism in politics, shark-like methods in the Stock Exchange and libertinism in private life are taken more and more for granted?

In the face of so many public scandals people call regularly for more regulation and control. But however important legal regulation and control are, they are no substitute for giving a basic ethical orientation. Still more rules for interaction and behaviour, still more laws, instructions and forms will certainly not help human beings, already under the stress of too much information and too much regulation, to find the way. Human beings today are not short of signposts here and there, telling them what they ought and ought not to do; it is rather that they so often do not know where they really ought to be going: they lack the main direction, the goal.

No, if modern society is to function, then we must not neglect the question of the intended goal and the 'ligatures' (as Ralf Dahrendorf puts it), the things that bind. And basic to human life is that which binds it to a direction in life, to values in life, to norms in life, to a meaning in life. Viewed across nations and across cultures, human beings have an elementary need for such basic ties (assuming that it has not been completely suppressed): they feel the desire to cling to something, to rely on something, to have a standpoint in such an incalculable, complex, technological world and in the confusions of their personal life. They need to follow some kind of guiding line, to have standards at their disposal, an idea of what the goal is: in short, to possess something like an underlying ethical orientation. And in an industrial society, where there is so much uncertainty because of too much information and disinformation, regardless of the undoubted importance of that open communication on all sides, which is so emphasized by social-psychology, and of models for alternative resolutions of disputes, proposed by lawyers, human beings will never behave in a truly humane way, in matters great or small, without having something that binds them to meaning, values and norms. (These must certainly never chain and shackle human beings, but should rather help and support them.) But what is the concrete meaning of underlying ethical orientation? Here it is precisely religious people who must ask themselves self-critically the following question:

Can human beings not also live a moral life without religion?

Now there is no doubt that, throughout the centuries, religions were those systems of orientation which formed the basis for a particular morality, gave it legitimacy and motivation and often sanctioned it by punishment. Indeed, it is incontestable that religions have been aware of this function for better and for worse, as everything human is aware of the great ambivalences of history. Better *and* worse: for only prejudice could overlook the huge contribution of the great religions to the spiritual and moral progress of the peoples of this world. However, at the same time we can hardly ignore the fact that they have also hindered this progress, indeed prevented it. Religions often proved themselves to be less driving forces of reform (as, for example, we find in the Protestant Reformation despite all the imbalances and weaknesses) than bastions of counter-reform and counter-enlightenment (as we find in the Vatican's high-handedness and obsession with power in the sixteenth and nineteenth centuries and again today).

Positive *and* negative things could, of course, be said about Judaism and Islam, Hinduism and Buddhism, Chinese Confucianism and Taoism, as well as about Christianity. In every one of the great world religions, along with a more or less triumphal success story (by and large better known to its adherents) there is also a chronicle of scandal (about which they would rather keep quiet). Indeed there were times, right up to the present, when, as the American psychologist Edgar Draper put it, '. . . institutionalized religion has never been particularly troubled by its bizarre adherents, wild movements, comic saints, lascivious Brahmans, paranoid preachers, disturbed rabbis, eccentric bishops or psychopathic popes. Nor has it seen fit to acknowledge character strengths in those heretics, reformers or rebels who opposed its teachings' (*Psychiatry and Pastoral Care*, Englewood Cliffs NJ 1965, p.117).

In these circumstances, can it be surprising that some enlightened contemporaries preferred rather to do without religion, which they equated with obscurantism, superstition and brainwashing the people; that today, while they no longer declare themselves militant atheists or agnostics, in every case they claim quite decisively to have a basic orientation and to be able to lead a moral life even without religion?

The religious person cannot escape the question: can only religious people really live in a truly humane, truly moral way? One's experience gives a negative reply: there are too many people in our society who are hardly religious at all, indeed clearly non-religious, yet who in terms of the requirements they make of themselves, set out to lead no less a moral life than believers, and who sometimes show more moral sensitivity in all possible (political-social) areas than certain 'pious' people (who usually have a fixation on sexual sins). Is, then, only the religious person to be able to have goals and priorities, values and norms, ideals and models, criteria for true and false? Can one make such a strong assertion in view of the character and work of an Ernst Bloch, an Albert Camus and a Bertrand Russell – to name only these three as typical representatives of major trends of the time? No, the highly moral philosophical thinker Immanuel Kant has spoken convincingly for many people: as rational beings, men and women possess a truly human autonomy which allows them to realize their basic trust in reality and to be well aware of their responsibility without believing in God. Many of the pioneers of human rights, particularly in England and France, were notorious freethinkers, whereas many opponents of human rights were believers in God, indeed notorious bigots, amongst them many bishops and popes.

So also today, many secular people exemplify in their lives a morality which orientates itself on the dignity of every human being; and according to present-day understanding, with this human dignity go reason and responsibility, freedom of belief and of religion, and the other human rights which have won through in the course of a long history, often laboriously enough against the established religions. And it is of the greatest importance for peace among nations, for international co-operation in politics, economics and culture, and also for international organisations like UNO and UNESCO, that religious people – be they Jews, Christians or Muslims, Hindus, Sikhs, Buddhists, Confucians, Taoists or whatever – do not dispute the fact that non-religious people, calling themselves 'humanists' or 'Marxists', can also, in their own way, represent and defend human dignity and human rights, a humane ethic. Indeed, both believers *and* non-believers are represented in what stands as Article 1 of the United Nations' Declaration of Human Rights, adopted on

10 December 1948 after the Second World War and its 55 million dead: 'All human beings are born free and equal in dignity and rights. They are endowed with reason and conscience and should act towards one another in a spirit of brotherhood.'

And from that comes also the right to religious freedom, which also includes, by logical necessity, a right to have no religion: 'Everyone has the right to freedom of thought, conscience and religion; this right includes freedom to change his religion or belief, and freedom, either alone or in community with others and in public or private, to manifest his religion or belief in teaching, practice, worship and observance' (Article 18).

All this, it appears, can be quite easily justified with human reason, without any principles of belief. As Immanuel Kant demanded to know in his programmatic work *What is Enlightenment?*, why should a human being not overcome the 'immaturity that is his own fault', the 'inability to make use of his understanding without being guided by someone else', and also use his understanding for the establishment of an ethics of reason? According to Kant, this inability is founded 'not in a lack of understanding, but of courage': 'Have the courage to make use of your own understanding!' For that reason many philosophical and theological ethicists today also advocate and defend a genuine human autonomy in all of a person's practical decisions, a moral autonomy which even Christian belief cannot simply cancel out. However, it is precisely the theological ethicists who at the same time draw attention to the danger of this moral autonomy, and rightly so. Why?

The difficulties reason has with ethics

'But from where do we get these standards that guide us, and where necessary, put us in our place? Science cannot teach us such norms?' So says a prominent scientist, the evolutionary biologist and President of the German Research Association, Hubert Markel. At the same time he warns not only against an anti-scientific fundamentalism, but also against a knowledge that is 'free of values', which no longer tells us 'why we ought to know what it teaches us' (*Die Zeit*, 8 September 1989).

What Theodor W. Adorno and Max Horkheimer analysed immediately after the Second World War as 'the dialectic of enlightenment' (1947), has today become to a large extent common property. It is in the nature of rational enlightenment itself for its reasonableness easily to turn into unreason. Not all scientific advances are advances for humanity. The restricted, particular rationality of science and technology is certainly not total, undivided reasonableness, a truly reasonable rationality. And a radical criticism of reason which literally goes to its roots by necessity attacks the very roots of this reason, and so easily undermines every reasonable legitimation of truth and justice. That is why Adorno and Horkheimer see the Enlightenment as being caught up in an inexorable process of self-destruction and why they call for a self-transcending enlightenment.

Indeed, the evil brought about by science and technology cannot simply be cured by even more science and technology. It is precisely scientists and technologists who today emphasize that scientific and technological thinking is indeed capable of destroying an ethic that is traditional and estranged from reality; and much that has spread in the modern age by way of immorality is not the result of ill will, but is rather an unwanted 'by-product' of industrialization, urbanization and secularization. But modern scientific and technological thinking have proved themselves, from the outset, as incapable of justifying universal values, human rights and ethical standards.

Indeed, even today, philosophy has difficulties in providing a foundation for practicable ethics: where should it get its criteria from in order to judge the 'interests' that lie behind all 'knowledge' (Habermas)? How should pure reason decide between true and illusory, objective and subjective, acceptable and reprehensible interests? How should it establish purely rational priorities and indeed limits? Up to now, it seems, the foundations that philosophy has provided for concrete norms have scarcely gone beyond problematic generalizations and utilitarian-pragmatic models which are generally too abstract for the average person and can in no way be generally binding. Do these generalizations and models not fail at precisely that point where a human being, in a specific case – and this is not all that unusual – is called upon to carry out an action which in no way serves either his interest or general happiness, which can rather demand of him an action against his interests, a 'sacrifice', and in an extreme case, even the sacrifice of his life?

There is a question which even Sigmund Freud, affirming his ethics on the basis of reason, was unable to answer: 'When I ask myself why I have always behaved honourably, to be ready to spare others and to be kind wherever possible, and why I did not give up doing so when I observed that in that way one harms oneself and becomes an anvil because other people are brutal and untrustworthy, then, it is true, I have no answer' (Letter to J. J. Putnam on 8 July 1915, quoted by E. Jones, *Sigmund Freud: Life and Work*, Vol. 2, London 1955, p. 465).

Can one therefore meet every danger of spiritual homelessness and moral waywardness with pure reason? Of course, in view of the lack of assistance from the sciences and technology and indeed philosophy, many people help themselves, each in his or her own way. The interest of many contemporaries in horoscopes, incomprehensible to those who know about astronomy, is due to this need for a basic orientation for future important decisions, as is the widespread thirst for serious and less serious 'aids to living'. But the great economic and technological problems of our time – from atomic energy through genetic manipulation and artificial insemination to the polluted environment and the North-South conflict – have become more and more political-moral problems (which is also the perception in the Club of Rome), and these problems are beyond the reach and also the power of any psychology and sociology. Today, when we can do more than we should, who can tell us what we ought to do? One is entitled to ask: can not *religions* perhaps contribute something here after all? However, religion also has its quite specific problems today.

The difficulties religion has with ethics

For a long time now, what perhaps some people in Islam and Hinduism today also feel to be a problem has been clear to many religious people – to Jews and Christians above all, but doubtless also to members of the Chinese religion. A first difficulty is that at the end of the twentieth century we can less than ever get fixed moral solutions from heaven or from the Tao, or derive them from the Bible or any other holy book. This does not contradict the transcendentally justified ethical commandments of the Bible, the Qur'an, the Torah, and of Hindu or Buddhist writings. But first, it must be admitted that, from the historical point of view, the concrete ethical norms, values, insights and key concepts of the great religions have, according to all historical research, developed in a highly complicated social and dynamic process. It is easy to understand that where life's necessities, human needs and imperatives appeared, human behaviour was subjected to regulations, priorities, conventions, laws, commandments, directives and customs; in short, precise ethical norms. And so much of what is proclaimed in the Bible as God's commandment can also be found in the Codex Hammurabi. That means that human beings have had to test and still have to test, again and again, ethical norms and ethical solutions in draft and model form, and often practise and prove them over generations. After periods of concession and acclimatization, the process finally leads to the recognition of norms to which people have grown accustomed in this way, but sometimes – if the time has completely changed – it can lead to their being undermined and dissolved. Are we perhaps living in such a time?

Religious people should also now bear in mind a second difficulty: for all problems and conflicts differentiated solutions 'on earth' must be sought and worked out. Whether as Jews, Christians, Muslims, or as members of an Indian, Chinese or Japanese religion, human beings are themselves responsible for the concrete fashioning of their morality. To what extent? To the extent that they too must proceed from their experiences, from the diversity of life, and must keep to facts. Even religious people cannot be excused from acquiring sure information and knowledge for all concrete problem areas, from sexual ethics to economic and state ethics. They must operate in all areas with factual arguments in order to arrive at verifiable aids to decision-making and finally also to reach practicable solutions. It is precisely religious people, often with their heads in the clouds, who today must say to themselves that they cannot call on a higher authority, however high that may be, in order to remove from human beings their autonomy in the world. In that sense there is certainly what was worked out at the time of the Enlightenment: an ethical self-legislation and self-responsibility for our self-realization and fashioning of the world, situated in the human conscience.

And religious people should take a third difficulty into account: in the face of the multi-layered, changeable, complex and often impenetrable reality of the technological society, even religions cannot avoid bringing scientific models to bear in order to examine this reality in as unprejudiced a way as possible for its factual regularities and future possibilities. Certainly not every average Christian, Jew, Muslim or Hindu needs to apply these scientific methods. Pre-scientific consciousness of precise ethical norms, in so far as it is present, of course retains its basic importance for a majority of believers today. And, happily, many people still act in particular situations in a 'spontaneously' correct manner, without having read a moral-philosophical or moral-theological tract. But it is precisely the misjudgments (with regard, for example, to war, race, the place of women or the importance of birth control) made by several religions in recent times which show that modern life has become too complex for one to be able to disregard, out of naive blindness to reality, scientifically secure, empirical data and perceptions in the determining of concrete ethical norms, particularly with regard to sexuality or aggression, but also with regard to economic or political power.

This means in positive terms that modern ethics is today dependent on contact with the natural and human sciences, with psychology and psychotherapy, with sociology and social criticism, with behavioural research, biology, cultural history and philosophical anthropology. In this respect, religions, their responsible leaders and teachers, should show no fear of making contact. It is precisely the human sciences which offer them a growing richness of relatively sure anthropological knowledge and information to act upon, and these can be used as verifiable aids for decision-making – even if they cannot replace final foundations and standardizations of the human ethos. For this is exactly where religions have their own contribution to make.

Religions – a possible foundation for an ethic

I firmly maintain that a human being without religion can also lead a life that is genuinely humane, that is to say with humanity, and in this sense moral; this is precisely the expression of a person's inner autonomy. But one thing those without religion cannot do, even if they were to accept unconditional moral norms for themselves, is to justify the unconditionality and universality of ethical obligation. It remains uncertain why I should follow such norms unconditionally, in every case and in every place – even where they run completely contrary to my interests. For what is an ethic worth in the last analysis, if it is not valid without all ifs and buts – unconditional, 'categorical' (Kant)?

One cannot, however, derive an unconditional, 'categorical' 'thou shalt' from the finite limitations of human existence. And even an independent, abstract 'human nature' (as justifying authority) could hardly provide an unconditional obligation to anything. Why should even the 'survival of mankind', not exactly threatened by any one individual alone, be a personal challenge to anyone in such a categorical way? Indeed, provided one is running no risks, oneself, why should not a criminal kill his hostages, a dictator violate his people, an economic group exploit a country, a nation start a war, a power block launch rockets in an emergency against the other half of humanity, if that happens to be in their own best interests, and if there is no transcendent authority which is unconditionally valid for all? Why should they all act unconditionally in a different way? Is the 'appeal to reason' sufficient in that case? And was not the Terror of the French Revolution justified in the name of the 'Goddess of Reason'?

Here in brief is the fundamental answer. Today – after Nietzsche's celebration of 'beyond good and evil' – one can no longer count on making the well-being of *all* people the measure of one's *own* action using a quasi-innate 'categorical imperative', common to all people. No, the categorical nature of the ethical demand, the unconditional nature of the 'thou shalt', cannot find its justification in a human being who is conditioned in so many ways, but only in the unconditional: an absolute which can provide an overall meaning which embraces and pervades the human individual even human nature, indeed the whole human community. That can only be the final, highest reality which, while it cannot be rationally proved, can be accepted in trust based on reason – whatever this reality is called, and however it is understood and interpreted in the different religions. At least for the prophetic religions, Judaism, Christianity and Islam, the only unconditional in all that is conditioned which can justify the unconditional nature and universality of ethical demands is the primal ground, the primal support, that primal goal of humankind and the world which we call God. This primal ground, this primal support and this primal goal does not mean that human beings are directed from without. On the contrary: having grounding, anchoring and orientation of this kind opens up the possibility for human beings truly to be themselves and act for themselves; it makes possible self-legislation and self-responsibility. Properly understood, theonomy is therefore not heteronomy, but rather the ground and guarantee of human autonomy.

But however the unconditionality nature of ethical demands is grounded in the different religions, whether they derive their demands more directly from a mysterious absolute, or a figure of revelation, from an old tradition or a sacred book, one thing is sure: religions can express their ethical demands with a completely different authority from a merely human one. For they speak with an absolute authority and are, in that very way, an expression of the 'oldest, strongest and most urgent desires of mankind' – to take up the atheist Freud's description of religion (*The Future of an Illusion*, in Complete Psychological Works of Sigmund Freud, Vol. XXI, London 1961, p. 30). And religions do not just express these desires simply with words and concepts, doctrines and dogmas, but also with symbols and prayers, rites and festivals – that is to say, both rationally and emotionally – for religions have the means of shaping the whole of a human being's existence – and this will be tested by history, adapted to a particular culture and given concrete form in the individual case.

But when one speaks, in this or any other way, of religion as the foundation of morality, one will hear the objection that religions are in no way in agreement themselves, that all their statements, not only about the absolute but also about the ethic of mankind, are different, even contradictory. Indeed one may ask: do religions not have totally different, mutually contradictory, theoretical and practical concepts to offer? We cannot avoid these questions in view of the contributions of the different religions to a world ethos.

Agreement and disagreement among religions: global commandments, vices, virtues

The disagreement between the great religions is so manifest that only someone who sees ghosts needs to fear as a reality in his lifetime the one single universal religion which many theoreticians strive for as the ideal. I personally believe in a possible unity between the Christian churches: in the lifting of all mutual excommunications in favour of a basic communion which would represent a reconciled variety, a unity in diversity. But I do not believe in the unity of the world religions representing different paths, all of which one can simultaneously follow without a second thought. Such a unity of world religions is not even necessary, so long as we also allow the other religions to be accepted as legitimate paths to salvation in themselves. What we need, however, and what I hope for, is peace between the religions; because without peace between religions there will be no peace between nations! And so it is important that, despite all the differences, we try to discern a precise agreement or at least convergence.

The various religions differ from one another in their teachings and writings as well as in their rites and institutions, and finally also in their ethics and discipline. The members of the various religions, for the most part, know only too well exactly where they have spectacular disagreements with one another in matters of practice. Christians, for example, know that Muslims and Buddhists should refrain from alcohol in any form; the latter know that, as a rule, Christians are allowed it. Jews and Christians know that Christians are allowed to eat pork; but the latter know that that is considered unclean by Jews and Muslims. Sikhs and high orthodox Jews may not cut their beards or hair, but Hindus and also Christians and Muslims can do as they wish. Christians may slaughter animals, Buddhists may not. Muslims may have several wives, Christians only one. And so on.

But are the members of the various religions so well informed about what they have in common precisely with regard to an ethic? By no means. Therefore what unites all great religions would have to be worked out in detail on the basis of the sources – a significant and gratifying task for the scholars of the various religions! But even at the present stage of investigation, some important areas of common ground can be emphasized. For – and this could be easily demonstrated – not only the prophetic religions of Near-Eastern, Semitic origin, but also the mystical religions of Indian origin aiming at unity with the Absolute, and also, finally, the religions of Chinese origin, steeped in wisdom and concerned about cosmic harmony, are in absolute agreement in some basic ethical imperatives:

Thou shalt not kill the innocent.

Thou shalt not lie or break promises.

Thou shalt not commit adultery or fornication.

Thou shalt do good.

These are all fundamental ethical demands on humanity. There is no doubt that an enormous amount could be achieved for the human race if all the great religions, their leaders and teachers, with all the means and possibilities at their disposal, were to lend their support to such common fundamental ethical demands, so that they became something like the basic pillars of a common fundamental world ethic.

If the part of the Jewish Decalogue aimed at one's neighbour has its direct or indirect parallels in all other religions up to and including Buddhism, so presumably also has the Christian catalogue of virtues and vices: as, for example, the seven main or cardinal sins as they have been enumerated since Gregory the Great: pride, envy, anger, greed, unchastity, immoderateness and (religious-moral) laziness; likewise also the four cardinal virtues taken over from the Greeks: wisdom, justice, bravery and moderation. Can one not find parallels in all the other great religions to these vices which Christianity condemns and these virtues it desires? Is there not something like universally prevalent sins, something like 'world vices', but, happily, also universally demanded virtues, something like 'world virtues'? Why should not the world religions find reconciliation in fighting world vices and promoting world virtues?

That could be easily confirmed from the perspective of the other religions. If, for example, self-sufficiency and lack of envy have a high status in Buddhism; if the world is to be respected, and not simply exploited; if human beings are to be seen as an end and never as a means; if knowledge means more than riches, and wisdom more than knowledge; if grief is no reason for despair, then one will certainly find parallels to these views on the Christian side – despite all the differences in the overall context. Or if the Muslim places especially high value on a sense of order and a striving for justice, if the virtues of courage and calmness occupy a particularly important place, while at the same time the Muslim is to distinguish himself by forbearance, humility and a spirit of community, one will certainly find parallels to all these virtues in Christianity and Judaism.

However, the last example in particular shows that in all religions one should always ask self-critically what the original nature of Christianity (of Islam, Judaism, Buddhism, etc.) really may have been. If we take the example just given, if we go back to the original Jesus of the Gospels, we can see that not only meekness and humility, but also prophecy and militancy, are part of Christianity. For this Jesus of the Gospels is as little understood as the prophet Muhammad, if he is seen only as a soft, gentle, unresisting, meek and humble figure, as he was in Pietism or in nineteenth- and twentieth-century Catholicism ('the sacred heart'!): a feeble image of Jesus, against which, rightly, the pastor's son Friedrich Nietzsche was not the only one to rebel in his youth. But the Gospel sources make it abundantly clear how very much Jesus of Nazareth was a thoroughly aggressive critic of the hierarchs and court theologians and how in his case, selflessness and self-awareness, humility and toughness, gentleness and aggression belong together. Could not, conversely, something of the selflessness, humility, gentleness and non-violence of Jesus of Nazareth be found in the militant prophet, general and statesman Muhammad? Neither the New Testament, the Qur'an nor the other holy scriptures have so far been examined with reference to global convergences of this kind.

At one point, indeed, the ethical convergence of the religions is expressed particularly strongly, namely in that supreme principle which for so long has been claimed exclusively for Jesus of Nazareth – the so-called 'golden rule'. This demands that one should treat one's fellows as one would want to be treated oneself. Today we know that the great Rabbi Hillel (*c.* 20 BC) was already familiar with this golden rule, although in a negative formulation, indeed that he even described it as the sum of the written law; in the Jewish Diaspora it is also found in a positive formulation. But K'ung Fu-tse, many hundreds of years before the birth of Christ, was also familiar with this golden rule in a negative form. And one can say that it is known in all the great religions in this or a similar form: do not do to anyone else what you would not like done to you. Or put positively: do to others as you would be done by. Kant's categorical imperative is basically a modernization and secularization of the golden rule.

Now that has also made it clear how very much true humanity represents a point of convergence in the great religions.

The *humanum* as a criterion of truth

At a UNESCO colloquium in Paris under the title of 'No world peace without religious peace', I defended the thesis that only a religion that promoted true humanity, *humanitas*, could be a true and good religion. The above reflections may serve to substantiate this thesis. For in all the convergences I have indicated, what matters in the end is that a human being should behave in a truly humane way towards fellow humans. In this sense, true humanity is indeed the prerequisite of true religion, and *humanitas* is the minimum demand made of all religions. Religions which in themselves do not make human rights a reality are no longer credible today.

But the converse has also become clear. True religion, in so far as it is directed in this form at one's fellow human beings, is the fulfilment of true *humanitas*. Religion (in the sense of the correct determination of the relationship of theonomy and autonomy, as described above) here shows itself as the optimal prerequisite for the realization of the *humanum*. If there is to be humanity among men and women as an unconditional and universal obligation, then there must be religion.

But what about the completely different theoretical and conceptual frames of reference of the various religions? Do they not put in question the convergences I have indicated? The answer to that can now be given: an ethic is concerned in the last analysis not with a variety of theoretical frames of reference but rather with what should or should not be done, quite practically, in life as it is lived. And with reference to this praxis, people who are religious in the best sense of the word from the various religions have always found and understood each other. Whether in fact the particular tormented, injured or despised human being is given help from a Christian or Buddhist, Jewish or Hindu stance, ought in the first instance to be immaterial to the person concerned. In this respect, common action and acceptance can certainly be arrived at, on both a smaller and a larger scale, even if the theoretical and implications of the various religions are completely different.

This is emphatically confirmed by a declaration which the 'World Conference of Religions for Peace' adopted in 1970 in Kyoto in Japan, and which expresses in exemplary fashion what a concrete, universal basic ethic, a world ethic of world religions, could be:

Meeting together to deal with the paramount theme of peace, we discovered that the things that unite us are more important than the things that divide us. We found that we have in common:

a conviction of the fundamental unity of the human family, of the equality and dignity of all men and women;

a sense of the sacrosanctity of the individual and his or her conscience;

a sense of the value of the human community;

a recognition that might is not the same as right, that human might cannot be self-sufficient and is not absolute;

the belief that love, compassion, selflessness and the power of the mind and inner truthfulness have, in the end, more power than hatred, enmity and self-interest;

a sense of obligation to stand on the side of the poor and oppressed against the rich and the oppressors;

deep hope that good will, in the end, will triumph.

Translated by Gordon Wood

Human Rights, the Rights of Humanity and the Rights of Nature

Jürgen Moltmann

I. The existence of human rights

In many civilizations, growing insight into the fundamental rights and duties of human beings went hand in hand with an awareness of the 'humanity' of human beings. Wherever there came to be a concept of 'the human being' as such, the rights of human beings, simply as human beings, were formulated too. These ideas are not exclusively Christian or European, although it was during the era of the Western 'Enlightenment' that the formulations of human rights made their way into North American and European constitutions, and although it is through these constitutions that human rights have acquired world-wide recognition today. Like other universal ideas – mathematics for instance – human rights have meanwhile become independent of the particular European history in which they developed, and now seem plausible and convincing simply on their own account, whenever people become aware that they are not merely Americans or Russians, black or white, men or women, Christians or Jews, but that they are first and foremost human beings. This means that there can be no copyright claims to human rights, neither Jewish and Christian, nor enlightened and humanist.

Today the nations are entering upon a common world history because they endanger one another mutually and mortally through the nuclear threat and because they share the equally mortal danger of the ecological crises. And the more this movement towards a shared future proceeds, the more important human rights are becoming, as part of a world-wide human society capable of averting these dangers. Human rights are therefore increasingly going to provide the universally valid, ethical framework for the evaluation and legitimation of 'human' policies, a framework on which there can be a general consensus. The recognition and the implementation of human rights for people everywhere will decide whether this divided and dangerous world is going to be replaced by a humane world-wide community that is in harmony with the cosmic conditions of life on earth, or whether human beings are going to destroy both themselves and the earth. Because the situation is so extremely dangerous, it must be established that human rights have an authority overriding all the particular interests of nations, groups, religions and cultures. Today particularist religious claims to absolute truth and the ruthless enforcement of particularist political interests are threatening the very existence of humanity itself.[1]

Yet the existing formulations of human rights are still not enough. We must work towards their expansion if human rights themselves are not to become a destructive factor in our world. It seems to me that human rights have to be extended in two directions. 1. The fundamental rights of humanity must be formulated; and 2. human rights have to be harmonized with the protective rights of the earth and other living things, and have to become a part of these.

The declarations of human rights which are in force in the United Nations today can be found, first, in the Universal Declaration of Human Rights of 1948 and, second, in the 1966 International Covenants on Human Rights (on Economic, Social and Cultural Rights, on Civil and Political Rights, the Optional Protocol). They certainly have very little binding force in international law, for the preamble says merely that human rights are a joint ideal to be attained by all peoples and nations. At the same time, since about 1970, civil rights movements in many countries have shown that these declarations have an astonishing power, and in the Conferences on Security and Co-operation in Europe (the first of which was held in Helsinki in 1975) their influence has increasingly come to prevail in international law in Western and Eastern Europe.[2]

Right down to the end of the Second World War, it was internationally accepted that the question of how a country treated its own citizens was a matter solely for its own sovereign decision. This is no longer the case today. Even though many states still reject 'interference in their internal affairs', the way a country treats its citizens is according to law a matter for all the other countries too, for today everyone falls under international law in so far as this protects human rights.

The categories and groupings of human rights already emerge from their history. Following the crimes of the Fascist dictatorships and after the Second World War, the North Atlantic states drew up 'charters' of individual human rights, over against the state and the forces of society. In their struggle against capitalism and class rule, the socialist states have emphasized economic and social rights. The people of the Third World, in the misery to which they have been reduced, are today demanding the right to existence, the right to live and survive. We can therefore distinguish the following groups: 1. protective rights – the rights to life, liberty and security; 2. freedom rights – the right to freedom of religion, opinion and assembly; 3. social rights – the right to work, to sufficient food, to a home, and so forth; and 4. rights of participation – the right to co-determination in political and economic life.[3]

The roots of these different human rights and the bond linking them is what Article 1 calls 'human dignity'. Human rights exist in the plural, but there is only a single human dignity. Human dignity is one and indivisible. It does not exist to a greater or lesser degree, but only wholly or not at all. Human dignity means the quality of being human, however the various religions and philosophies may define this. At all events, human dignity makes it illegitimate to subject human beings to acts which fundamentally call in question their quality as what Kant called 'determining subjects'. Because human dignity is one and indivisible, human rights are a single whole too, and cannot be added to, or subtracted from, at will.

But to base human rights on human dignity also shows the limitations and perils of their inherent anthropocentricism.[4] Human rights have to be harmonized with the rights of nature – the earth from which, with which and in which human beings live. Human dignity is not something that separates human beings from all other living things. It is merely a special example of the dignity of all the living – the dignity of all God's creatures, to put it in Christian terms. Human dignity cannot be fulfilled through human rights at the cost of nature and other living things, but only in harmony with them and for their benefit. Unless human rights come to be integrated into the fundamental rights of nature, these rights cannot claim universality. On the contrary, they themselves will become factors in the destruction of nature, and will then also ultimately lead, paradoxically enough, to humanity's self-destruction.

In the ecumenical discussions after the Second World War we can see interesting shifts of emphasis. From 1948 (the Assembly of the World Council of Churches in Amsterdam) up to about 1960, discussion centred on the question of religious liberty – until people realized that religious liberty can be implemented only in the context of other individual human rights. The Conferences on Security and Co-operation in Europe, as well as conditions in Turkey, show that it is still important to demand both today. Step by step, religious liberty, together with individual human rights, is also being recognized in the countries with state ideologies and state religions.

Since about 1960 questions about human rights in the social and economic sectors have come to the fore. Racism, colonialism, dictatorship and class rule are being attacked as serious infringements of human rights. The rights to personal freedom cannot be protected in a world of flagrant political injustice and economic inequality. Only economic and social rights put people in a position to implement freedom for themselves. The ecumenical consultation in St Pölten, Austria, in 1971, was a milestone in the history of discussions between the Christian churches about human rights, because here representatives of the people of the Third World talked and were listened to. Today, in the industrial countries, the ecological discussion is at the centre of interest. It sets human rights imperatively in the framework of the conditions in which the earth itself lives, and in the framework of the cosmos which sustains life.

At the end of the 1970s the major churches then issued their own declarations on human rights. In 1976 the World Alliance of Reformed Churches made a statement on the theological foundation of human rights, in 1977 came the declaration of the Lutheran World Federation on theological perspectives on human rights, and in 1976 a working paper was issued by the papal commission *Iustitia et Pax* on 'The Church and Human Rights'. Unfortunately there has as yet been no joint Christian declaration on this topic.

If I am right, only the declaration of the World Alliance of Reformed Churches has taken up a stance on the problems facing us today with regard to human rights and the rights of nature, although the Alliance, too, has failed to expand the actual framework in which human rights have to stand if they are really to be universal and supportive of life.

I shall now attempt a systematic survey, seeing human rights as a spiral which presses in the direction of universality, one group of human rights pointing forward to the next:

1. No individual human rights without social rights.
2. No human rights without humanity's right to protection from mass annihilation and genetic change, and the right to survive in the succession of the generations.
3. No economic human rights without ecological duties towards the rights of nature.
4. No human rights without the rights of the earth.

II. Individual and social human rights

'We hold these truths to be self-evident, that all men are created equal, that they are endowed by their Creator with certain unalienable rights', says the American Declaration of Independence. If this means all human beings, irrespective of sex, race, religion, health, etc., then it means every single person. Every human being is a person, and as person is equipped with 'unalienable rights'. The American constitution and the constitutions of the French Revolution, with their maxims about the liberty and equality of all human beings, also of course already posed the fundamental problems of modern constitutional states: how to mediate between individual rights to liberty and the protective rights of society in the sphere of social security and economic provision. And this is where the political conflict between the liberal democracies and socialism arises.

In the 'prophetic' religions, Judaism, Christianity and Islam, the liberty and equality of all human beings is based on belief in creation, about which the American Declaration of Independence also speaks. Human beings – all human beings, every human being – enjoy their dignity because they are made in the image of God.[5] Men and women are intended to live in this relation to God. It gives their existence its inalienable transcendent dimension of depth. In the relationship to the transcendent God people become persons whose dignity must not be infringed. In claiming to be human institutions, the institutions of the law, the state and industry become in duty bound to respect this personal dignity of all human beings. They would destroy themselves if they were to treat human beings as objects, things, marketable goods, 'underdogs' or working tools. They would lose their legitimation.

In the lordship myths of many peoples it is only the ruler who is venerated as 'God's image on earth', 'the Son of Heaven' and 'the Son of God'. The ruler is 'the shadow of God and human beings are the shadow of the ruler', says the Babylonian rulers' code. But according to Jewish, Christian and Islamic faith in creation, it is not any ruler who is created as God's image on earth. It is 'the human being' – all human beings and every human being. This means that all men and women are kings or queens, and that no one must dominate anyone else. The *Sachsenspiegel*, or 'Saxon Mirror' (a thirteenth-century private codification of laws), already said this (*Landrecht* Book 3, Art. 42): 'God has created and formed human beings in his own image and has redeemed them through his own anguish, the one like the other . . . According to my view,' says the author, 'I am unable to understand why anyone should be [the property] of another.'

In the political history of Europe, belief that everyone was created in the image of God, and respect for the liberty and equality of all, led to the democratization (in principle) of all rule exercised by one human being over others. Every exercise of power has to be legitimated towards other human beings. Ruler and ruled must at all times together and to the same degree be recognizably 'human beings'. This means that all citizens are equal before the law, to which even rulers are subject. A democratic way of arriving at political decisions, the temporal limitation of the commission to rule, the control of rule through the separation of powers and through popular representation, the binding of government to the constitutional charge and, not least, a large measure of popular self-determination and communal self-administration: all these things have become political ways of respecting the fact that every human being is created in God's image and that all human beings enjoy a common dignity.

Yet the movement for freedom in European and North American history was one-sided in stressing only individual rights over against political rule, and neglecting people's rights to social equality, and their economic security. It was the fault of Western liberalism to overlook the social dimension of liberty, which is to be found in the solidarity of human beings with one another. This was also an error in religious history in the West, from Augustine onwards: it is not the individual, bodiless soul which is God's image; it is the human being together with other human beings, since God created human beings 'male and female', according to the biblical story of creation.

Although individual and social rights have different intellectual roots and have still never been gathered together in a single document, individual and social rights belong logically together, and whenever they are implemented they involve one another. Human sociality has in principle the same dignity as human personhood. The person is not there 'before' the community, nor is the community 'before' the person. Persons and communities necessitate and condition one another mutually, and complement one another, in the same way as human individuation and socialization. Consequently no preference can in principle be given to individual rather than to social rights, although this is always what is assumed in the Western world. The rights of persons can be realized only in a just society, and a just society can be realized only on the basis of personal rights. The freedom of persons can be developed only in a free society, and a free society grows up only out of the freedom of persons. There can be no 'free choice of work' without 'a right to work'. 'The right to work' presupposes 'the free choice of work', if human beings are to live as free men and women.

It is pointless and absurd when the democratic West and the socialist East bewail the violation of individual rights on the one hand or the infringement of social rights on the other. It is much better for both sides, and more helpful for humanity generally, if the two sides learn from one another and find a balance between their ideas about the freedom and equality of human beings.

III. Human rights and the rights of the human race

Human rights have hitherto been formulated only in the context of persons and societies, but not yet with a view to humanity itself, although the concept 'human being' logically includes the concept 'humanity'. Has humanity as a whole rights and duties too? This has not been very much thought about, because people always presupposed that the life and existence of humanity was a matter of course – divinely willed and a fact of nature.

1. But ever since 1945, with Hiroshima, it has become increasingly evident that the human race is mortal and that its time has a time-limit. This has been made clear through the super-powers' commitment to the nuclear deterrent system, and through the production of chemical and biological means of mass annihilation. Humanity's very existence is under deadly threat through the 'crimes against humanity' which are possible at any time through the unleashing of wars with atomic, biological and chemical weapons.[6] Yet humanity should survive and wants to survive. This fundamental affirmation of human life is implied in every declaration on human rights. It is now time for us also to formulate and recognize publicly humanity's right to existence and survival, for this is something which human beings can deny. There are even specific situations in which the rights of humanity have unconditional priority over the particular rights of certain classes, races and religion, and when all special interests, however justifiable they may be, have to be subordinated to humanity's right to exist. Even 'the class struggle' as a way of bringing about the liberation of the oppressed makes sense only if it belongs within the framework of the survival of humanity.[7] Even the absolutist claim of particular human religions must be subordinated to the right of humanity to exist and to survive, because that claim could otherwise lead to the suicide of the human race.

Because the threat to humanity proceeds from the power of the state, which is in possession of atomic, biological and chemical weapons, the limitations of state power must be more closely defined, in the context of humanity as a whole. To threaten potential enemies with the methods of mass annihilation which can lead to the extinction of the human race goes beyond the right of any country which claims to be 'humane'. The different countries do not merely have a duty towards their own citizens. They have a duty towards humanity as a whole as well. They do not merely have to respect the human rights of their own citizens. They have to respect the rights of the citizens of other countries too, for human rights are indivisible. National foreign policies based on rivalry with other countries and systems must give way to a 'world-wide domestic policy' which is committed to the survival of humanity, a policy which will serve the mutual promotion of life and the security of all. This means that international human solidarity in the ending of mutual threats has to take priority over loyalty towards our own nation, race, class or religion. Individual states and communities of states have human duties towards the right of the human race to live and survive.

2. If human dignity forbids us to infringe anyone's 'quality as determining subject' or to destroy it permanently, this applies not merely to individuals but also to coming generations and the human race as a whole. Modern genetic engineering and the new reproduction medicine have made it possible not only to cure hereditary diseases, but actually to breed different human beings through 'eugenics'.[8] Prenatal diagnostics enable the evolution through selection of new human generations. Manipulations of the germ cells can fundamentally alter the genome of the human race. Of course therapeutic interventions are permissible as long as they conduce to healing. But manipulations designed to breed living things that lack the human quality of being 'determining subjects', and manipulations designed to breed so-called supermen, destroy the essence of human beings and therefore human dignity as well. If by protecting human dignity the state has also taken on the duty of protecting every human life, then it has the additional duty of protecting the humanity of human life in this and coming generations. Otherwise it would lose its legitimation. The 'optimizing' genetic intervention in the species human being (or whatever name may be given to 'advantageous' genetic interference with the human species) belongs just as much to the new category of crimes against humanity as the annihilation of what are supposed to be the 'unfit' and the destruction of races declared to be inferior. There is a new racist application of evolutionary theory and eugenics to the future of the human race which annihilates its dignity and humanity. The genetic self-destruction of humanity is a new and increasing danger, which stands side by side with the continuing nuclear threat.

3. 'Humanity' is not merely made up of all the people living in the cross-section of any single time. It also means people in the longitudinal section of all the times, in the sequence of human generations. At any single time in any single area there are always different generations living together and looking after one another: parents caring for their children, the young for the old. Because the human race exists in the temporal sequence of the generations, up to now a natural 'contract between generations' has ensured the survival of the human race – a contract which, because it is natural, was considered a matter of course. The law of inheritance conferred a degree of justice between the generations, so that there came to be a certain equalization of the chances in life enjoyed by those living earlier and those living later. Today this unwritten contract between generations is threatening to break down, and this breakdown can have deadly consequences for the human race. In the industrial nations we are in process of using up in a single generation the greater part of the non-regenerative sources of energy (oil, coal, wood, and so forth) and in our public budgets we are leaving the generations to come horrific mountains of debt which they will one day have to pay off. We are using up the profits of industrial production in our own time and are pushing off the costs on to times in the future. We are producing huge rubbish dumps which coming generations will have to 'dispose of', although we know quite well that it is very difficult to dispose of chemical waste and that nuclear waste cannot be 'disposed of' at all, but will have to be kept under surveillance until the year 3000 or 10000, according to the decay time of the material.[9]

But the human race can survive only if the contract between generations creates justice between the generations in which humanity exists in time. Since today the contract can be irrevocably broken, it must be formulated and publicly codified. In our present situation we have to pay particular attention to the rights of children and the right to live of coming generations, because children are the weakest links in the generation chain, while coming generations have as yet no voice at all and are therefore the first victims of the collective egoism of generations today.

IV. Economic rights and ecological duties

Human dignity also means actually being able to lead a life of human dignity. This involves certain minimum presuppositions, socially and economically – protection from hunger and sickness, for example, and the right to work and to personal property. Recently the protection of the natural environment has also come to be counted among the minimum guarantees of personal human dignity. We can think about and develop economic rights and political rights to liberty in an analogous way. In the political sphere, it contravenes the dignity of human beings to be made mere objects of state power; and in the same way it is inconsistent with human dignity if people are degraded economically to mere working tools and pure purchasing power. If they are to live out their 'quality as determining subjects' in the economic sector too, human beings must be given a just share in work, property, food, protection and social security. The concentration of capital goods and other means of production, as well as foodstuffs, in the hands of a few, and the suppression and exploitation of the many, is a severe violation of human dignity. A worldwide economic situation which allows millions to die of hunger is unworthy of humanity and is in Christian terms an infringement of God's glory, which is to be found in human beings, as his image.

If it is all human beings, not any special races or classes, who enjoy the dignity of being created in God's image, so that they are 'free and equal', this must lead to a democratization of economic life which will correspond to political democratization. The trade union movements and workers' rights to co-determination in factories and commercial enterprizes are steps in this direction. But the world-wide democratization of economic life is proving particularly difficult, because here the interests of capital are in alliance with the interests of the nations of the First World. Yet it can be shown that unless there is more justice through a democratization of the world-wide economy, there is going to be an economic and ecological catastrophe for humanity generally; for the growing exploitation and indebtedness of countries in the Third World is compelling people there to cut down their rain forests and to exploit their fields and pasture until they turn into dust bowls and deserts; and this means destroying large areas of what provides the foundation for the life of humanity as a whole.

The fundamental economic rights of each and every human being are bound up with particular fundamental ecological duties. The body of basic economic rights cannot be increased *ad infinitum*, in the wake of a rapidly increasing population and the growing demands of particular nations, for, as everyone knows, ecological limits are set to economic growth on this earth. The human struggle to survive cannot be pursued at nature's expense, because the ecological collapse of nature would mean the end of all human life on earth. Economic rights must therefore be harmonized with the cosmic conditions of the nature of the earth where human beings live and increase. This means that ecological justice between human civilization and nature must match economic justice between the people in a society, between human societies, and between the generations of the human race. But up to now the only correspondences have been ecological and economic *in*justice: the exploitation of human workers was precisely matched by the exploitation of natural resources. The exploitative relationship of human beings to nature will cease only when the exploitative relationship of human beings to one another ends and is reversed. This is not merely a moral judgment. It is a counsel of wisdom as well, for today the technical means of exploitation have been increased to the point when they can totally destroy the natural foundations of human life. It is therefore stupid for the sake of short-term profits to annihilate the foundations on which one's own life is based in the long run – stupid because suicidal.

Many people therefore see the protection of nature from destruction by human beings as being one of the minimum guarantees of individual human dignity. But then we can speak only of the individual's right to an unharmed environment, in the way that we can talk about the individual's right to freedom from bodily harm. And in this case nature is perceived only as 'environment', existing for the sake of human beings themselves. But this viewpoint is sufficient to preserve nature from the aggression of human beings. Nature must be protected from human beings for her own sake, which means for the sake of her own dignity. The very same modern anthropocentricism which is inherent in earlier formulations of human rights and human dignity has also led to the narrow and dangerous view of nature as 'human environment'. The protection of nature with its plant and animal species, the protection of the conditions of life on earth, and the protection of earth's equilibriums must be assigned a status in modern state constitutions and international agreements which corresponds to the status assigned to human dignity.[10] Does nature, and do other living things, have a dignity analogous to the dignity of human beings?

V. The rights of the earth and the dignity of its living communities

If the world is seen merely under the aspects of private law, it evidently consists only of 'persons' and 'things', just as according to the modern view of the world (held since Descartes) there are only subjects and objects. But are animals really only 'things' in relation to the human persons who can possess and use them? Are they not living beings, capable of feeling pain, and human beings' fellow creatures? And do they not then have rights of their own and a certain subjectivity which human beings ought to respect?

Ever since the beginning of modern Western civilization we have become accustomed to viewing nature as the environment *for us*; it is related to ourselves. We look at all other natural beings with an eye solely to their utility value where we are concerned. Only human beings are there 'for their own sake'. Everything else is supposed to be there 'for the sake of human beings'. This modern anthropocentricism has robbed nature of its soul and made human beings unembodied subjects. Pre-modern views of the world, the views held in antiquity, saw the whole world as 'ensouled'. Aristotle still talked about the soul of plants, the soul of animals and the soul of human beings, as well as the soul of the world, all these souls being differentiated and yet related, in a single complex. The Old Testament talks the same language (Gen. 1.30; Isa. 11). Post-modern views of the world, on the other hand, assume that human beings are a unity of body and soul, their bodily needs and the relations to other natural living things prompting the development of the notion of a cosmic community, of which human beings are an integral part.

Both these attitudes indicate that the modern cleavage between person and thing, subject and object, does justice neither to the natural community or symbiosis in which and from which human beings live on earth, nor to the bodily existence of human beings themselves. If this cleavage is rigorously forced through with modern methods, nature's symbioses will be destroyed and human bodilyness with them. Ultimately speaking, modern anthropocentrism is deadly for human beings themselves.[11] Of course we can hardly go back to the cosmocentrism of ancient times in the way we see the world and life, even if some modern thinkers see this as a way out of the deadlocks of the modern world; for anthropocentrism is the very basis of modern industrial society, whereas cosmocentrism was the foundation of the agrarian society of the pre-industrial age. But modern anthropocentrism can be fitted into the conditions for life on earth and into the symbiosis, or community, of all living things in a way that is not a nostalgic and 'alternative' flight from industrial society but which will reform it until it becomes ecologically endurable for the earth, and is integrated into the early fellowship of the living.

Yet a community of life shared with all other living beings on this earth will remain a dream if it is not realized in a community of all the living based on law. An earthly community of this kind would have to open the human community based on law for the rights of other living things and the rights of the earth, fitting the human community into the universal laws of life which apply to the whole earth. This means respecting the earth, plants and animals for themselves, before weighing up their utility value for human beings. Just as human dignity provides the source for human rights, so the dignity of creation is the source of the natural rights of other living things and the earth. A general declaration on animal rights which corresponds to the General Declaration of Human Rights of 1948, harmonizes with it and where necessary corrects it, ought to be part of modern state constitutions and international agreements. A draft of a declaration of this kind has existed since 1977.[12]

An animal is not a person in the human sense, but it is not a 'thing' or a product either. It is a living being, with rights of its own, and it needs the protection of public law. Respect for this fact means putting an end to industrial, hormone-controlled 'meat production', and going over to a way of keeping animals which will be in accordance with the requirements of their species. It will also mean reducing as far as possible the millions of animals used in animal experimentation and replacing them by other techniques, such as simulators. In the United States at least seventeen million animals are 'expended' in laboratory experiments every year; in Europe one million were used in the chemical centre in Basel alone. More and more people are quite rightly asking: 'Do the practical benefits of animal experimentation outweigh the moral costs?' (*Newsweek*, 16 January 1989). The moral costs are undoubtedly evident in the growing indifference towards other life, whether it be animals, embryos or other people, an indifference the backlash of which is inescapably felt in our own lives. In view of the deadlocks of the industrial societies, with their hostility to nature, we must rediscover the position and role of human beings in the warp and weft of life on earth, and go on to make human rights part of the wider, comprehensive rights of nature, if we want to survive.

As I see it, this requirement is self-evident. But it poses a serious question to the religions which have provided the foundations for modern Western civilization. Has the Jewish and Christian tradition not conceded human beings God-like privileges towards all other living things, ever since the biblical accounts of creation? Are not human beings alone God's image on earth, and destined to rule over the earth and its other living things? Did this anthropology not provide the basis for developing human rights especially in the West? This is indeed the way we have to see the matter, for this is what has been maintained for centuries by churches and theologians. And yet it is not the whole truth, for the special destiny of human beings applies only *within* the community of all creatures, which they are intended to respect, as Psalm 104 makes clear. We can talk about the special dignity of human beings on the presupposition that the dignity of all other beings as creatures is recognized – not otherwise. As images of the Creator, human beings love all their fellow-creatures with the

Creator's love. If they do not, they are not the image of the Creator and Lover of the living. They are his caricature. That is why the special rights to life and existence enjoyed by human beings are valid only as long as these human beings respect the rights of the earth and other living things.

According to the biblical traditions there is a community based on law which goes beyond the human community of law – a community of the earth and human beings rooted in the special rights of God the Creator to what he has created. We find this in the enactments about the sabbath: the weekly sabbaths and the regular sabbatical years are given to human beings and the animals belonging to the human household. But 'the sabbath of the earth' is assigned a special, emphasized importance (Lev. 25 and 26). According to Ex. 23, Israel is to leave the land uncultivated every seventh year, and is not to harvest it 'so that the poor of your people may eat'. According to Lev. 25, an ecological purpose is added to this social one: 'So that the land may keep its great sabbath to the Lord.' In the seventh year the earth is to lie fallow so that it can renew itself. This is the earth's right. The person who keeps 'the sabbath of the earth' will live in peace, but anyone who disregards it will be visited by drought and hunger for having destroyed the earth's fertility. According to the ancient biblical story, God gives Israel up to Babylonian captivity for seventy years 'until the land – God's earth – had enjoyed its sabbaths' (II Chron. 36.20f.). Today the earth's right to regeneration is largely disregarded. Chemical fertilizers and pesticides force the earth into a permanent, unnatural fertility. Irreversible erosion is the consequence, and human famines become unavoidable. Anyone who disregards the rights of the earth is mortally threatening coming generations and the survival of humanity.

VI. The world religions in the forum of human rights[13]

Because present life and the future survival of humanity depend on the observance of human rights, the rights of humanity and the rights of nature, the world religions will also have to subordinate themselves to the world's preservation. In all the different religions there is nothing higher than truth. Today the religions will really only become 'world' religions when they begin to integrate themselves into the conditions of life and the growing community of law of this single world, and are prepared to surrender their particularist claims to absoluteness in favour of universalism. The religions must learn to respect religious liberty as a human right, and in this framework to behave tolerantly towards one another, and to be ready for dialogue. This also means that they have to subordinate their own legal codes – the Torah and the Sermon on the Mount, the laws of the church and the Shari'a, the ethics of Hinduism and Confucianism, and so forth – to the minimum demands of the rights of men and women, humanity and nature. If contradictions were to be maintained this would make the religious communities the enemies of the human race.

On the other hand the further development of the rights of men and women and of humanity is dependent on creative contributions by the various religious world views. Up to now, formulations of human rights have been based on the tradition of modern Western humanism, which in its turn grew up in the context of the Jewish-Christian religion. As we have seen, this culture is strongly anthropocentric in emphasis. Judaism, Christianity and Islam have therefore been called 'historical religions' over against the Asiatic and African 'nature religions'. And it is true that they are concerned with human hope and historical progress, whereas the nature religions cultivate the wisdom of equilibrium and adjustment. They have therefore also been called 'prophetic religions' and 'book religions', compared with the directly sensory spirituality of the Indian and Chinese religions, which have close ties with nature. However we may describe these very general differences, where the ecological problem of modern society is concerned, the balance between progress and equilibrium, the harmony between human history and nature, and the unity of person and nature is of vital importance. Today the inter-religious dialogue will have to direct its attention towards these vital human questions if it is to be of practical value for both the Western and the Eastern religions, and for humanity.

Translated by Margaret Kohl

Notes

1. Cf. J. Moltmann, *Creating a Just Future*, London and Philadelphia 1989. Also L. S. Rouner (ed.), *Human Rights and the World's Religions*, Boston University Studies in Philosophy and Religion IX, Notre Dame, Ind. 1988.

2. Cf. W. Heidelmeyer (ed.), *Die Menschenrechte. Erklärungen, Verfassungsartikel, Internationale Abkommen*, Paderborn 1972.

3. Cf. W. Huber and H. E. Tödt, *Menschenrechte. Perspektiven einer menschlichen Welt*, Stuttgart 1977; J. M. Lochman (ed.), *Gottes Recht und Menschenrechte. Studien und Empfehlungen des Reformierten Weltbundes*, Neukirchen 1976; text and preparatory papers in A. O. Miller (ed.), *A Christian Declaration on Human Rights*, Grand Rapids 1977.

4. The modern concept of 'human dignity' comes from Renaissance humanism. Cf. Pico de la Mirandola, *Oratio de dignitate hominis* (1486), Zürich 1988. It is linked with the anthropocentrism of modern anthropology: 'I have set thee at the centre of the world . . .' (10). But as long as the special dignity of human beings is defined by separating them from animals and by excluding other living things, the concept serves human domination over nature and becomes the energy of life. This anthropocentrism, which is so hostile to nature, can be overcome only if human dignity is theologically defined: it is based on the fact that men and women are the image of God. It then stems from the relationship in which God puts himself to human beings, and can do without demarcations and exclusions.

5. On the *imago Dei* doctrine cf. L. Scheffczyk (ed.), *Der Mensch als Bild Gottes*, Wege der Forschung CXXIV, Darmstadt 1969; J. Moltmann, *God in Creation*, London and New York 1985, Chap. IX, 'God's Image in Creation: Human Beings', 215ff.

6. As far as I am aware, it was the Assembly of the World Council of Churches in Vancouver in 1983 which first talked about 'crimes against humanity', meaning crimes against the whole human race.

7. M. Gorbachov, *For the Sake of Preserving Human Civilization*, Moscow 1987. Lenin already said that 'Situations may arise in which the concern of the whole of mankind has to be given precedence before the class interests of the proletariat.'

8. This is recommended by P. Singer, *Practical Ethics*, Cambridge 1979. For a contrary view cf. C. Altner, *Leben auf. Bestellung? Das gefährliche Dilemma der Gentechnologie*, Freiburg 1988.

9. Cf. *Our Common Future. The Brundtland Report of the World Commission on Environment and Development*, London 1987. On the question of the contract between generations cf. P. Saladin and C. A. Zenger, *Rechte künftiger Generationen*, Basel 1988.

10. G. M. Teutsch, *Lexikon der Umweltehik*, Göttingen 1985.

11. A. Auer, *Umweltpolitik. Ein theologischer Beitrag zur ökologischen Diskussion*, Düsseldorf 1984, however, believes that it is possible to maintain an anthropocentrism which is ecologically tolerable (203ff.). The alternative is not a cosmocentrism such as K. M. Meyer-Abich recommends in *Wege zum Frieden mit der Natur. Praktische Naturphilosophie für die Unweltpolitik*, Munich 1986. The answer is rather to decentralize human culture and to incorporate it harmoniously into a single web with nature.

12. The German law on the protection of animals in the version of 18 August 1986 (BGBL I 1320) introduces the concept of the 'fellow-creature': 'The purpose of this law is to protect the life and well-being of animals out of human responsibility for the animal as a fellow-creature. No one is permitted to cause an animal pain, suffering or damage without reasonable grounds.' Cf. A. Lorz, *Tierschutzgesetz, Kommentar*, Munich [3]1987. This presupposes the theological framework of Creator, creature and fellow-creature in a community of creation, and is probably unprecedented in a secular statute.

13. Cf. L. S. Rouner (ed.), *Human Rights and the World's Religions* (n.1).

Contributors

LEONARD SWIDLER received an STL from the Catholic Theology Faculty of the University of Tübingen in 1959 and a PhD in history and philosophy from the University of Wisconsin in 1961. Since 1966 he has been Professor of Catholic Thought and Interreligious Dialogue at Temple University, Philadelphia, Pennysylvania. He is author or editor of over 40 books and 130 articles, and Co-founder (1964) and Editor of the *Journal of Ecumenical Studies*. His books include: *Freedom in the Church* (1969), *Aufklärung Catholicism 1780–1850* (1978), *Religious Liberty and Human Rights* (1986), *A Catholic Bill of Rights* (1988), *After the Absolute: The Dialogical Future of Religious Reflection* (1990).

EUGENE B. BOROWITZ is the Sigmund L. Falk Distinguished Professor of Education and Jewish Religious Thought at the New York School of Hebrew Union College-Jewish Institute of Religion where he has taught since 1962. In twelve books and numerous articles he has expounded a new understanding of Judaism he terms Covenant Theology. He is one of liberal Judaism's leading theologians and he was the first Jew to serve as President of the American Theological Society. Rabbi Borowitz is the Editor of *Sh'ma, a journal of Jewish responsibility*, a magazine of Jewish social concern he founded in 1970.

Publications include *Choices in Modern Jewish Thought* (1983), *Liberal Judaism* (1984) and contributions to Haim Cohn, *Human Rights in Jewish Law* (1984); Louis Jacobs, *A Jewish Theology* (1973); David Novak, *The Image of the Non-Jew in Jewish Law* (1983); Shubert Spero, *Morality, Halakha and the Jewish Tradition* (1983). His most recent book is entitled *Exploring Jewish Ethics*.

KNUT WALF was born in Berlin-Dahlem in 1936. After studying philosophy, theology, jurisprudence and canon law in Munich and Freiburg he was ordained priest in West Berlin in 1962. He gained his doctorate in Canon Law at the University of Munich in 1965 and was engaged in pastoral ministry in West Berlin from 1966 to 1968. He gained his post-doctoral qualification in Munich in 1971. From 1972 to 1977 he was a university lecturer in Church Law and Church-State Law as well as Director of the Canonical Institute in Munich. From 1977 he has been Professor of Canon Law at the Catholic University of Nijmegen, Holland, and also Professor at the Theological Faculty in Tilburg. More recent publications in the field of church law and theology are: *Menschenrechte in der Kirche* (with M. Pilters), Düsseldorf 1980; *Stille Fluchten – Zur Veränderung des religiösen Bewusstseins*, Munich 1983; *Einführung in das neue katholische Kirchenrecht*, Zürich-Einsiedeln-Köln 1984; *Kirchenrecht*, Düsseldorf 1984; *Vragen rondom het nieuwe kerkelijk recht*, Hilversum 1988; *Westliche Taoismus-Bibliographie / Western Bibliography of Taoism*, Essen 1989; *Tao für den Westen – eine Hinführung*, Munich 1989. He is a permanent collaborator with *Orientierung* (Zürich).

ROGER GARAUDY was born in Marseilles in 1913. He is an associate Professor of Philosophy and Doctor of Arts of the Sorbonne and Doctor of Science of the USSR Academy. From 1945, he was Member of Parliament for Tarn, then for Paris. He was Vice-President of the National Assembly from 1956 to 1958 and Senator for the Seine from 1959 to 1962. A leading member of the French Communist Party, he was formerly Director of the Centre for Marxist study and research and, as such, organizer, in France and throughout Europe, of 'Christian-Marxist dialogues'. Among his principal works, most of which have been translated into several languages, are: *Perspectives de l'homme* (^{3}1961); *D'un réalisme sans rivages* (1963); *Clefs pour Karl Marx* (1967); *Parole d'Homme* (1975); *Appel aux vivants* (1979); *Promesses de d'Islam* (1981); and his memoirs, *Mon tour du siècle en solitaire* (1989). At present, he is Director of the International Institute for Dialogue between Civilizations.

ABDULLAHI AHMED AN-NA'IM is Associate Professor of Law, University of Khartoum, the Sudan and Ariel F. Sallows Professor of Human Rights, College of Law, University of Saskatchewan, Canada, from August 1988 to June 1990. He is a Muslim who believes that Muslims have a right and duty to live in accordance with the precepts of Islam. However, he believes that some aspects of the historical formulations of Islamic Law (Shari'a) can and should be drastically reformed prior to their modern application. He has explained and documented his approach to Islamic law reform in a forthcoming book entitled *Toward an Islamic Reformation*, Syracuse 1989. Other publications include an English translation with an

Introduction of *Ustadh* Mahmoud Mohamed Taha, *The Second Message of Islam*, Syracuse 1987; *Sudanese Criminal Law: The General Principles of Criminal Responsibility* (in Arabic), Omdurman 1986.

BITHIKA MUKERJI was educated at Allahabad University. Her first thesis was written under the guidance of Professor A. C. Mukerji, a leading neo-Vedantist of his time. She was invited to lead a seminar and participate in a graduate programme in Bossey, Geneva during the year 1972–73. She was at McMaster University from 1973–77, writing her second thesis on *The Ontology of Bliss*. She was invited to attend the Zweites christlichefernöstliches Religionsgespräch der Stiftung Oratio Dominica in November 1984. The topic of her paper was 'Advaitic Experience and Cosmic Responsibility'. Dr Mukerji taught in the Department of Philosophy in the Benares Hindu University, from where she retired in December 1984. Her publications include *Neo Vedanta & Modernity*, Varanasi, India 1983; *The Hindu Tradition*, New York 1988.

SULAK SIVARASKA is Visiting Professor to a few Thai, American and European universities. He mainly teaches Buddhism and philosophy. In 1983 he was one of the four Buddhists invited to attend the World Assembly of the World Council of Churches at Vancouver. He is Chairman of the administrative committee of the Thai Inter-Religious Commission for Development and Director of the Santi Pracha Dhamma Institute. His latest publications in English are *Siamese Resurgence*, *A Buddhist Vision for Renewing Society, Religion and Development*, and *A Socially Engaged Buddhism*.

KARL-JOSEPH KUSCHEL was born in 1948. He studied German and theology at Bochu and Tübingen universities. He graduated in 1972 and gained his doctorate in theology in 1977. From 1973 to 1983 he was Assistant Lecturer, and from 1981 has been Academic Adviser at the Institute for Ecumenical Research at the University of Tübingen and Lecturer in the Catholic Theological Faculty. The main focus of his research is the interdisciplinary research field of theology and religion. Within this framework he holds interdisciplinary seminars with literary scholars. His publications include:

Jesus in der deutschsprächigen Gegenwartsliteratur (introduction by Walter Jens) (1978); *Heute noch knien? Über ein Bild von Edouard Manet* (1979); *Stellvertreter Christi? Der Papst in der zeitgenössischen Literatur* (1980); *Gottesbilder-Menschenbilder. Blicke durch die Literatur unserer*

Zeit (1985); *Weil wir uns auf dieser Erde nicht ganz zu Hause fühlen. Zwölf Schriftsteller über Religion und Literatur* (1985). He has also edited or co-edited a number of books.

HANS KÜNG was born in 1928 in Sursee, Switzerland. From 1960 he was professor of Fundamental Theology in the faculty of Catholic Theology in the University of Tübingen, and from 1963 Professor of Dogmatic and Ecumenical Research. Since 1980 he has been unattached Professor of Ecumenical Theology and Director of the Institute of Ecumenical Research in the University of Tübingen.

His publications include: *Justification* (1957); *The Council and Reunion* (1960); *Structures of the Church* (1962); *The Church* (1967); *Infallible?* (1970); *On Being a Christian* (ET 1977); *Does God Exist?* (ET 1980); *Eternal Life?* (ET 1984); *Christianity and the World Religions* (with J. van Ess, H. von Stietencron and H. Bechert) (ET 1987).

JÜRGEN MOLTMANN was born in Hamburg in 1926 and is a member of the Evangelical-Reformed Church. He studied at Göttingen, was professor at the Kirchliche Hochschule Wuppertal from 1958–63, at Bonn from 1963–67, and now holds a chair for systematic theology at Tübingen. He is president of the Gesellschaft für Evangelische Theologie. His publications include: *Prädestination und Perseveranz* (1961); *Theologie der Hoffnung*, 12th ed. 1985 (ET *Theology of Hope*, 10th ed. 1983); *Perspektiven der Theologie*, 1968 (ET [selections] *Hope and Planning*, 1971); *Der Mensch*, 4th ed. 1979 (ET *Man*, 1974); *Die ersten Freigelassenen der Schöpfung*, 6th ed. 1976 (ET *Theology of Joy*, 3rd ed. 1982 [in US as *Theology of Play*]); *Der gekreuzigte Gott*, 5th ed. 1986 (ET *The Crucified God*, 8th ed. 1985); *Kirche in der Kraft des Geistes*, 1975 (ET *The Church in the Power of the Spirit*, 2nd ed. 1981); *Zukunft der Schöpfung*, 1977 (ET *The Future of Creation*, 1979); *Trinität und Reich Gottes*, 2nd ed. 1985 (ET *The Trinity and the Kingdom of God*, 2nd ed. 1986); *Gott in der Schöpfung*, 3rd ed. 1987 (ET *God in Creation*, 1985); *Gerechtigkeit schafft Zukunft*, 1989 (ET *Creating a Just Future*, 1989); *Der Weg Jesu Christi*, 1989 (ET *The Way of Jesus Christ*, 1989).

Members of the Advisory Committee for Ecumenism

Directors

Hans Küng	Tübingen	West Germany
Jürgen Moltmann	Tübingen	West Germany

Members

Anna Marie Aagaard	Aarhus	Denmark
Donald Allchin	Canterbury	Great Britain
Johannes Brosseder	Königswinter	West Germany
Robert Clément SJ	Hazmieh	Lebanon
John Cobb	Claremont, CA	USA
Avery Dulles SJ	Bronx, NY	USA
André Dumas	Paris	France
Herman Fiolet	Hilversum	The Netherlands
Bruno Forte	Naples	Italy
Alexandre Ganoczy	Würzburg	West Germany
Manuel Gesteira Garza	Madrid	Spain
Adolfo González-Montes	Salamanca	Spain
Catharina Halkes	Nijmegen	The Netherlands
Alisdair Heron	Erlangen	West Germany
Michael Hurley SJ	Belfast	Ireland
Walter Kasper	Tübingen	West Germany
Karl-Joseph Kuschel	Tübingen	West Germany
Emmanuel Lanne OSB	Chevetogne	Belgium
Pinchas Lapide	Frankfurt/Main	West Germany
Hervé Legrand OP	Paris	France
Peter Lengsfeld	Münster-Hiltrup	West Germany
Joseph Lescrauwaet MSC	Louvain	Belgium
George Lindbeck	New Haven, CT	USA
Jan Milic Lochman	Basel	Switzerland
Antonio Matabosch	Barcelona	Spain
Harry McSorley	Toronto, Ont.	Canada
John Meyendorff	Tuckahoe, NY	USA
José Miguez Bonino	Buenos Aires	Argentina
Ronald Modras	St Louis, MO	USA
Daniel O'Hanlon SJ	Berkeley, CA	USA
Wolfhart Pannenberg	Gräfelfing	West Germany
Otto Pesch	Hamburg	West Germany
Alfonso Skowronek	Warsaw	Poland
Heinrich Stirnimann	Fribourg	Switzerland
Leonard Swidler	Philadelphia, PA	USA
Stephen Sykes	Cambridge	Great Britain
Lukas Vischer	Bern	Switzerland
Willem de Vries SJ	Rome	Italy
Maurice Wiles	Oxford	Great Britain
Christos Yannaras	Athens	Greece

CONCILIUM

CONCILIUM

CONCILIUM

Concilium Special Offer: We are offering to existing subscribers, new subscribers, and special groups, an opportunity to buy back issues at greatly reduced prices. Some titles are in very short supply and will not be available again.

For a list and prices of back issues, please write to the publisher who handles your subscription:

SCM Press Ltd
26–30 Tottenham Road
London N1 4BZ
Fax: 01–249 3776
(071 *after 6 May 1990*)

Trinity Press International
3725 Chestnut Street
Philadelphia
Pa. 19104
Fax: 215–387–8805

Subscribe to Concilium

We are pleased to announce that from 1990 onwards *Concilium* will be published by Trinity Press International in the United States and SCM Press in Britain.

TPI and SCM Press are one company, spanning the world; an organization which is committed to publishing the best works of ecumenical theology in single, joint-imprint editions which are available without complication all over the world.

SCM Press, which celebrated its 60th birthday in 1989, is well-known for its wide range of theological publications; it has long been publishing the works of major theologians associated with Concilium: Edward Schillebeeckx, Hans Küng, Gustavo Gutierrez, Jürgen Moltmann and many others. Trinity Press International is a new development, founded in 1989 but already a major force in publishing in the USA.

All existing subscriptions placed with T. & T. Clark will be fulfilled by TPI/SCM Press. US and Canadian subscribers will in future be mailed directly from the TPI organization in Philadelphia; UK and other subscribers throughout the world will be mailed from SCM Press in London.

For the best and promptest service, new subscribers should apply as follows:

US and Canadian subscribers:

Trinity Press International, 3725 Chestnut Street, Philadelphia PA 19104
Fax: 215–387–8805

UK and other subscribers:

SCM Press, 26–30 Tottenham Road, London N1 4BZ
Fax: 01 (after 6 May 1990 071) –249 3776

Existing subscribers should direct any queries about their subscriptions as above.

Subscriptions rates are as follows:

United States and Canada: $59.95
United Kingdom, Europe, the rest of the world (surface): £34.95
Airmail to countries outside Europe: £44.95

Further copies of this issue and copies of most back issues of *Concilium* are available at $12.95 (US and Canada)/£6.95 rest of the world.

Trinity Press International, Philadelphia / **SCM Press,** London

Some recent and forthcoming titles

A Black Future?
Jesus and salvation in South Africa
Ronald Nicolson

Can traditional Christian doctrines of salvation and atonement still hold when faced with a situation like that in South Africa where Christianity oppresses Christians? What realistic hope does Christian theology offer for blacks?

00120 X   paper $18.95   £9.50

Global Theology
The role of faith in the present world crisis
Rex Ambler

Sets the profound doubt prompted by our current life-style and values against a religious faith struggling to survive in the face of that doubt. The deepest human questions explored against the background of today's world.

02434 X   paper $7.95   £4.95

Marx and the Failure of Liberation Theology
Alistair Kee

In the first sustained criticism of liberation theology from the left, Alistair Kee surveys its leading proponents and accuses them of being too conservative in their theology, not taking into account Marx's criticism of religion.

02437 4   paper $21.95   £15.00

Still Living with Questions
David E. Jenkins, Bishop of Durham

A striking demonstration of the consistency of David Jenkins' thought over twenty years, this major collection of occasional writings is about God; the caring professions; world faiths; church, worship and sacraments; and the authority of faith.

02439 0   paper $16.95   £10.50

The Heart of the Global Village
Technology and the new millennium
William A. Charland Jr

Based on personal experience in Canada, the USA, Britain and Africa, this survey of the current technological and social changes which will usher in the next century forms an agenda for the churches.

02438 2   paper $9.95   £5.95

Jewish Law from Jesus to the Mishnah
E. P. Sanders

Taking further his re-examination of Jewish law in *Paul and Palestinian Judaism*, Professor Sanders re-examines Jesus' conflict and the law, and considers the practicality of implementing purity laws, the Pharisees, the Mishnah and many other related topics.

02102 2   cased $29.95   £35.00